THE MASTERY OF INNOVATION

A Field Guide
to Lean Product
Development

THE
MASTERY
OF
INNOVATION

A Field Guide
to Lean Product
Development

Katherine Radeka

CRC Press
Taylor & Francis Group
Boca Raton   London   New York

CRC Press is an imprint of the
Taylor & Francis Group, an **informa** business

CRC Press
Taylor & Francis Group
6000 Broken Sound Parkway NW, Suite 300
Boca Raton, FL 33487-2742

© 2013 by Katherine Radeka
CRC Press is an imprint of Taylor & Francis Group, an Informa business

No claim to original U.S. Government works

Printed in the United States of America on acid-free paper
Version Date: 20120618

International Standard Book Number: 978-1-4398-7702-9 (Hardback)

Library of Congress Cataloging-in-Publication Data

Radeka, Katherine.
 The mastery of innovation : a field guide to lean product development / Katherine Radeka.
      p. cm.
 Includes bibliographical references and index.
 ISBN 978-1-4398-7702-9
 1. Production planning. 2. New products--Management. 3. Lean manufacturing. 4. Industrial efficiency. I. Title.

HD30.28.R293 2013
658.5'038--dc23   2012022421

Visit the Taylor & Francis Web site at
http://www.taylorandfrancis.com

and the CRC Press Web site at
http://www.crcpress.com

To my life partner,

Gene Radeka

Contents

SECTION III   Lean Product Development
to Make the Right Products

**SECTION IV   Lean Product Development
to Make Products Better, Faster, Cheaper**

SECTION VI   The Path of Innovation Mastery

Acknowledgments

My gratitude goes first to all the people who participated in the Lean Product Development Benchmarking Study. They allowed me to wander their halls, peer into their labs, and question them relentlessly. This book would not be possible without their generosity.

I am also indebted to the pioneering researchers in the field of Lean Product Development. Dr. Durward K. Sobek of Montana State University has been a mentor and a friend for the past eight years. Drs. Allen Ward, Jeffrey K. Liker, and James Morgan at the University of Michigan also provided us with insights into Toyota's Product Development System. Thanks to Mary Poppendieck, who is responsible for getting me into all of this in the first place with her groundbreaking work on Lean Software Development, and to Dr. H. Thomas Johnson, who first introduced me to Lean Thinking when I was an MBA student at Portland State University.

This study would not have been possible without the connections I made at Lean Product & Process Development Exchange conferences, with help from my fellow board members Michael N. Kennedy, Rich Gildersleeve, and Jim Huntzinger, and our event coordinator, Sharon Brown and her team. Dr. Ahmed Al-Ashaab at Cranfield University in the UK, Dr. Göran Gustafsson at Chalmers University in Sweden, Dr. Torgeir Welo at NTNU in Norway, Dr. Eric Rebentisch at MIT in the United States, and Dr. Pat Lynch of Business Alignment Strategies guided the research plan in its early days and provided referrals to help me deepen the pool of companies that I studied far beyond my own clients and friends.

Finally, thanks to my husband and business partner, Gene Radeka, for helping me organize a vast array of handwritten notes into a clear, coherent picture of the current state of Lean Product Development. He was my traveling companion, co-interviewer, sounding board, first reader, strategic analyst, finance director, and best friend on this journey.

Introduction

The mastery of innovation is the ability to get great ideas out into the market so that they can deliver value for paying customers, with consistency and predictability. A lot of companies have been able to get some good products to market. Masters of innovation build a track record of delivering great products to the market with every new product launch. They deliver great ideas better and faster than their competition.

The product developers and leaders profiled in this book have found that the mastery of innovation is the mastery of Lean Thinking. Lean helps them get more of what they want, and less of what they don't want. When they consistently approach product development from this perspective, they discover that they have mastered the process of innovation.

Over the past two years, I have gone to the labs, engineering offices, conference rooms, and executive suites that bring new products to life, with Lean Thinking to maximize value and minimize waste. These pages tell the stories of companies working to solve product development problems with Lean ideas, as well as the Lean Champions who made it possible.

I visited big companies, small companies, and microcompanies in different industries and geographic regions. I found a diverse group of companies who were willing to help me demonstrate that Lean Thinking dramatically improves product development performance.

LEAN PRODUCT DEVELOPMENT IS THE MASTERY OF INNOVATION

These companies get their ideas to market faster, develop more of their ideas into products, smoothly transfer new products into operations, reach breakeven sooner, and have lower costs from development through end of life. At their best, they deliver products that their customers adore. They have mastered innovation through Lean Thinking.

If you think you know what Lean is this may surprise you. You may have heard the word "Lean" used to describe outsourcing, "offshoring," budget cuts, and layoffs. You may have seen Lean programs come and go at your company. You may have even seen Lean successes in other parts of the business that could not be replicated in the R & D labs.

You may think that Lean only applies in manufacturing. You may think that Lean is for the automotive industry, for companies that still do their own manufacturing, for large companies, for other companies—but not for you and your company. You may think that innovation is too creative to be seen as a process at all—much less a Lean process.

If you have these thoughts, the experiences described in this book will give you a new perspective on the mastery of innovation.

Lean Product Development can make you more innovative as an engineer or scientist. It can make your teams more innovative, and it can make your company more innovative. The more people you can get engaged, the more powerful it will be.

This book will show you how product developers have used Lean Thinking to solve their most pressing problems and their customers' most pressing problems, so that they can get their ideas to market faster, better, and cheaper. They have mastered the process of innovation.

MY JOURNEY

I first learned about Lean as an MBA student, studying with H. Thomas Johnson at Portland State University in the mid-1990s. Dr. Johnson was best known then for a book he wrote, called *Relevance Lost,* about the perils of management accounting systems. When seeking alternative management systems, Dr. Johnson became interested in two companies: Scania and Toyota. He wanted to understand how Lean Thinking at Toyota and platform development at Scania had led to their breakthrough performance.

At the time, Lean emphasized the toolkit of Lean Manufacturing: the seven wastes of manufacturing, kanbans to manage work-in-progress inventory, error-proofing to reduce defects, 5S (Sort, Shine, aSsign a Home, Systematize, Sustain) to organize shared workspaces and one-piece flow. As a software developer, these ideas were interesting to me but not directly applicable. But I still remember a lecture that Dr. Johnson gave about Scania's platform strategy for commercial vehicles, where he showed that modular designs helped them eliminate waste, lower cost, and optimize their production processes.

By 1999 I had become a coach for software development teams at Hewlett Packard, teaching the rapid development practices that we call "Agile" today. In 2002, I attended OOPSLA, a major software development conference. I saw that Mary Poppendieck of 3M would give a presentation on "Lean Software Development" during a session that I had open. I decided to see what she had to say.

That day, Mary explained why Agile methods worked from a Lean perspective. She showed how they eliminated the common wastes in software development. She demonstrated that the small batch sizes of Agile Development eliminated the huge waste that happens when you deliver a software package that does everything it's supposed to do perfectly— except that the users hate it because it was not at all what they had in mind. I took away a lot of ideas that I was eager to try with my teams, and I sought out more information on Lean Development.

I found two papers and two dissertations that came out of a University of Michigan research program that studied the Toyota Product Development System. Drs. Allen Ward and Jeffrey Liker directed this program, while graduate students Durward Sobek and James Morgan did most of the primary research and wrote their dissertations to report the results. I began experimenting with these ideas as I coached software program managers.

In late 2003, another team brought Allen to my site. His early visits fired up the leadership team with his frank talk about the dangers of conventional wisdom in product development, which were plainly visible in our own processes. I wanted to be a part of this effort so much that I weaseled my way onto the team, even though I was supposed to be working with a different division altogether.

In late June of 2004, Allen was on his way to visit us in Vancouver, Washington, when his small plane got caught in a thunderstorm. He never made it.

We were shocked and saddened, but determined to move ahead.

Dr. Durward Sobek, now a professor at Montana State University, became our primary guide. We would have moved him to Vancouver if he was willing, and I still remember my work with him and that team as one of the most intense learning experiences of my life.

I spent the next year adapting a training program that Allen had left behind so that we could build Lean Problem-Solving skills within our product development teams, as well as assisting with the development of an online training course to raise awareness about Lean. I taught the new problem-solving workshop solo for the first time to a team in

Barcelona—an American female software engineer teaching Japanese business practices to a group of Spanish male mechanical engineers.

A year later, I faced a decision point: I could spend the next years of my career helping other teams at HP as I had done since 1999, or I could help other companies use Allen's methods. I decided to help as many companies as I could, but first I wanted to learn more about how companies were adapting Lean Product Development to meet their needs.

THE REAL PLACE

Allen's work had taught me an important lesson about Lean Thinking: If you truly want to understand something, you need to "go-and-see" it for yourself.

Lean thinkers call this "going to the *gemba*"—a Japanese word that, loosely translated, means "the real place." You have to see the real place for yourself. As human beings, our eyes, ears, and other senses record much more information than we could ever write down to share with someone else.

If you have the opportunity to go to the real place, it is your responsibility to describe and model it as accurately as possible for those who could not get there. For my first experiments with Lean Product Development, the real place was the development lab right in front of me: the problems and challenges, the waste that surrounded the developers, the customer value they tried to deliver. We improved the things that worked and learned from the things that didn't.

In the fall of 2005, I left HP. A week later, I began a journey to go to the real places where other U.S. companies were experimenting with Lean in product development. I drove over 11,000 miles from Oregon to Kentucky and back, visiting over 40 companies. At the time, I didn't know what I was going to see or what I would do with the knowledge once I had it. To my great regret, I captured little explicit knowledge from that trip. But I learned a lot that I began to share with the companies I met:

- Teams that studied and modeled themselves after the Toyota Product Development System got better results than those who tried to use Lean Manufacturing analogues in product development.

- Waste is almost entirely hidden in most product development organizations, making it harder to eliminate.
- Just as conventional methods of manufacturing generate a lot of excess waste, conventional methods of product development generate a lot of excess overhead.

Even back then, a few companies did Lean Product Development well enough to achieve breakthrough product development performance. They had mastered the process of innovation.

In 2010, after five years of serving as a guide to companies as they adapted Lean Product Development, I decided it was time to go back to the real place, this time with a mission: to see how product development leaders had interpreted "Lean Product Development" for themselves to help their companies get their best ideas to market faster.

I found 63 companies willing to talk with me about what Lean Product Development means to them and the results that they have seen. Of those, more than 20 were willing to share their stories with you.

YOUR MISSION

As you read these stories, reflect upon what they have done—not to copy them but rather to use them as the basis for your own solutions (or countermeasures, as Lean Product Developers prefer to say) to the problems that you face in product development right now.

Most of the companies in this book started with one person willing to do some experimentation and take a few risks to start down the path of mastery.

You don't even have to call it "Lean" to make it work for you.

You can simply call it the "mastery of innovation."

Section I

Lean Product Development: The Mastery of Innovation

1

Lean Product Development: The Mastery of Innovation

The ability to innovate is only worth something if those innovations generate value. A lot of great ideas never make it out of concept development, don't get to the market ahead of competitors, or lose all their profitability to post-launch quality problems. Lean Product Development is the ability to get ideas to market faster, by maximizing value and minimizing waste every step of the way.

Lean Product Development companies deliver the right products to the market at the right time and the right price. The specific benefits that companies report include:

- **Greater schedule predictability.** Teams can accurately predict how long products will take to move through the major phases of development so that they hit launch dates consistently. Products do not get stuck in redesign loops that cause delays late in development.
- **Shorter development time.** Teams can deliver products at least 50% faster after they have learned how to use the practices of Lean Product Development than they could using "industry standard" product development practices. In practice, the first group of Lean Product Development programs usually goes more than 30% faster, reaching 50% on the second round of programs. Companies on their third round can go even faster if market needs require it, or they may invest their new capacity in more product development programs.
- **Increased R & D capacity.** People spend much less time on tasks that create no value, freeing up time to spend on value-creating innovation.

- **Lower costs throughout the product life cycle.** Not only do products developed in this way cost less to develop but they also have lower costs in manufacturing and post-sales support.
- **Less uncertainty.** Product development teams have a better understanding of what they know, what they don't know, and what they need to do to close the gaps in their knowledgment. There are many fewer nasty surprises in late product development and afterward.
- **Products that meet customers' needs more completely.** Teams have the ability to learn more about customer needs and the ability to translate that knowledge into products with the right benefits at the right price.

Lean Product Development companies earn higher profits and build stronger competitive advantage.

At the same time, Lean Product Development practices give the most innovative people in your organization—the technical wizards and marketing geniuses—more time and space to do what they do best, with better support structures to help them do it. Libraries of reusable knowledge ensure that they don't waste any brainpower on reinvention. Improved risk management and decision-making practices make it possible for development teams to delay decisions to give the innovators more time to work out the details of their ideas without putting the schedule at risk. Reduced project management overhead, better documentation practices, and more productive meetings ensure that they stay focused on the next innovation.

THE DEFINITION OF LEAN PRODUCT DEVELOPMENT

Lean experts commonly define Lean as "eliminate waste," but this definition is not sufficient in product development. Product developers are the ones who determine the maximum value a product can deliver. Some parts of Lean Product Development focus explicitly on understanding and delivering maximum value.

When people eliminate waste in product development, they have to make sure that they don't also compromise their ability to deliver value. For example, ideas that teams pursue and then abandon are not waste—as long as they have captured what they've learned, shared it, and used it to come up with better ideas. A failure in manufacturing is almost always waste; a failure in early product development is a valuable learning experience.

Lean Product Development is

Product developers systematically solving problems to maximize value and minimize waste across the entire system.

Every part of this definition is important.

A ***product developer*** is anyone who participates in the product development process. Since product development involves many different functional areas, we may find product developers anywhere. We usually find them in engineering, design, advanced development, research labs, strategic marketing, procurement, quality, and manufacturing engineering. Others may also get involved: Sales reps build useful relationships with customers; operators may have the best understanding of manufacturing capabilities. Customer support representatives and field technicians get detailed information about current product performance and reliability. Lean is not something that an expert does for a team, and it's not something that requires any special certification. It is something that product developers do themselves.

A ***problem*** is anything that gets in the way of progress toward an objective. Many organizations stigmatize problems to the point that all the problems are hidden, and all projects are on track—until they're late. Lean Product Development organizations say that "no problem" is a problem! They embrace problems and actively seek them out. Lean systems and tools make problems visible as soon as possible. Once we see a problem, we can begin to solve it.

Systematic problem solving goes beyond solving the surface problem to understand why the problem happened in the first place and fix the root cause so that it does not come back again. While many engineers see the value in this, they claim that there is no time in the product development schedule for this, even though they have experienced the waste that short-term fixes create. They are right: Conventional methods for managing product development place no value on systematic problem solving or the knowledge it creates. Lean Product Development organizations value systematic problem solving so much that they expect every product developer to use it on a daily basis to solve problems.

We solve problems so that we can maximize value and minimize waste across the entire system. We don't optimize one part of the system at the expense of another. We may add waste someplace to remove more waste someplace else. In order to do this, we need to have a good understanding of customer and business value, and we need to learn to see the waste in product development.

WE ALREADY DO ALL OF THIS—HAVE WE MASTERED INNOVATION?

Conventional wisdom creates more waste than value. Many companies' efforts to increase innovation and speed up product development set a vicious cycle in motion that actually slows down product development (Figure 1.1). Managers put pressure on teams to be more creative and go faster, overloading them with more work than they can realistically do. In early product development, teams can go faster and alleviate overload by spending less time on problem analysis, testing, and supplier qualification and by making key design decisions without exploring alternatives.

All of these shortcuts come back to haunt these managers in late development when one problem after another adds delay to the schedule. If the problem is bad enough or the teams continue to take shortcuts to relieve the pressure of overload, defects escape, customers find them, and the product is plagued by post-production engineering change requests that take time and energy away from future products. Since few product development groups can just hire more staff, their people get even more overburdened. Product development gets slower and more unpredictable.

FIGURE 1.1
The vicious cycle of waste in product development.

SYSTEMATIC PROBLEM SOLVING
AND COUNTERMEASURES

To build a Lean Product Development organization, a solid foundation of systematic problem solving must be put in place. People need confidence that they have the skills to solve problems and the support to use those skills. People in positions of leadership need to ensure that their behaviors pull the organization toward systematic problem solving rather than fire fighting, expediting, and overload.

SYSTEMATIC PROBLEM SOLVING METHODS

The *scientific method* is the original systematic problem-solving method: Develop a hypothesis, design an experiment, run the experiment, and adjust the hypothesis based on the results. Many product developers use the scientific method in their daily research and development work, but few of them think to apply these methods to the value streams that surround them. When we think scientifically about the flow of work, we make product development waste visible so that we can eliminate it.

Plan–Do–Check–Act (PDCA) is the classic rapid learning cycle. Walter Shewhart developed this cycle in the United States in the 1930s and perfected it during WWII. W. Edward Deming popularized it, first in Japan in the 1950s and then in the United States in the 1980s. In the 1990s, Jim Womack and the Lean Enterprise Institute incorporated it into the fabric of Lean Thinking. Toyota and many other companies have developed their own versions of PDCA to ensure that all the steps get done well.

In the early 2000s, Dr. Allen Ward developed *LAMDA* (Look-Ask-Model-Discuss-Act). It is a systematic problem solving method tailored for engineers and scientists to leverage their strengths and address their weaknesses. Most of the companies in this book use LAMDA as their systematic problem-solving method for product development.

LAMDA: Systematic Problem Solving for Product Development.

COUNTERMEASURES

All of the Lean tools, including the tools in this book, are ***countermeasures.*** A countermeasure is by definition an interim solution, which helps us remember to review it periodically to see if it's still working, and to improve it if we can. We always have the ability to replace it with a better countermeasure later.

Toyota developed some innovative countermeasures to solve the problems it encountered and to help eliminate waste. The Toyota Product Development System serves as a model for Lean Product Development, just as the Toyota Production System is the model for Lean Manufacturing. But in product development, Toyota is only part of the story.

Other leading product development organizations have countermeasures to leverage, even though they don't use the word "Lean" themselves to describe their practices. Google has groundbreaking methods for gathering tactical customer knowledge. Agile software teams in a variety of companies have conducted many experiments that contribute to less wasteful project management. Apple's Steve Jobs was the quintessential innovation master, able to integrate deep customer and technical knowledge into products that customers love.

When reading the rest of this book, or any other book that makes recommendations about product development, it is important to remember that the solutions are countermeasures designed to fit a specific situation at a specific company. To decide whether or not they may help you, first use systematic problem solving to ensure that you need to solve the same problem; then, test out the counter-measure to see if it works in your environment.

As a result, the product development teams solve the same problems over and over again, without understanding why their interim fixes appear to work. They rush through early product development to hit aggressive milestones and then get stuck when things don't work out. They spend hours updating product development program schedules, specifications, and budgets that are obsolete the moment they are printed. They pack their calendars with meetings to communicate status information and then spend the meeting time trying to catch up on the endless flow of e-mail. In trying to go faster, they just create more waste.

To get out of this cycle, product development leaders need to understand how to recognize value in product development, and how to see the waste that blocks innovation. They can get some new ideas from companies that have figured out how to clear away all of this clutter to free up space and time for the systematic problem solving that leads to innovation.

HOW DOES LEAN PRODUCT DEVELOPMENT DELIVER RESULTS?

Lean product development works because it clears away all of this clutter to give engineers and other product developers the time they need for systematic problem solving to maximize value and eliminate waste.

The less waste there is inside product development, the more time product developers have to solve customer, technical, and business problems systematically to maximize value. We specifically eliminate the wastes of unproductive meetings, unclear and revisited decisions, overloaded resources, reinvention, design loopbacks, excess documentation, and project status reporting. These sources of waste bleed away the organization's technical capacity minute by minute and hour by hour in activities that contribute nothing to the finished product.

In product development, this is especially important because of the costs of time switching. Engineers can take as long as 15 minutes to recover from an interruption, even if that interruption was only a minute or two. Knowledge workers of all kinds need uninterrupted time to focus on their work. E-mail, chat, "drive-by" conversations, and meetings all interrupt the flow of work, making it more difficult to get anything done. Many people work early in the morning or late at night to get this uninterrupted time, even if that's not the best time for people to make complex decisions. Lean Product Development incorporates the principles of cadence, pull, and flow to significantly improve the amount of uninterrupted, productive, value-creating time that engineers have to develop products.

The less waste there is in our product designs, the more reliable they are, and the less they cost to make. Complexity and newness adds cost and risk that our customers may not be willing to pay for. Even in the most bleeding-edge industries, there are opportunities to capture what we know about our technology in ways that make it easier to build knowledge from one product to another, and to incorporate that knowledge into our newest products. This reduces the risk of costly design loopbacks, while reducing overall product cost. Most of the time, the customer does not notice the shared technology and would not care if he or she did. Customers do notice products that are more reliable and less costly.

THE ENGINE OF KNOWLEDGE CREATION

When we eliminate waste in our processes and in our products, we set in motion a virtuous cycle that frees up time and energy for the thing that matters most: how to deliver the best product to the right customer, at the right price, at the right time.

This virtuous cycle is the engine of knowledge creation (Figure 1.2). All product development organizations create knowledge, but few have the capacity to learn. They waste time learning the same things over and over, and they miss opportunities to use their knowledge to drive innovation.

Lean product development unlocks the value from all of this knowledge by making it easier to create, capture, share, and use. We can use this knowledge to ensure that we don't repeat the same mistakes over and over, and we can leverage this knowledge to form the basis for innovative products that have high value and low risk. The incremental investment it takes

FIGURE 1.2
The virtuous cycle of knowledge creation in product development.

to capture and share our product knowledge returns compounded value when product development is fast, predictable, reliable, and innovative.

When your company has gained the ability to capitalize on your organization's knowledge while eliminating everything that stands in the way of using that knowledge to deliver great products, you have mastered innovation.

Discussion Questions

- What are some of the attributes that drive customer value for your company's products?
- Of the benefits of Lean Product Development in this chapter, which ones are most important for your company right now?
- What waste do you see in your organization's product development process?

Next Actions

- ☐ Check your calendar to see how much time you spent in meetings over the past week. What happened during those meetings? If your colleagues spent most of the meeting time on e-mail, what could you do to improve the effectiveness of those meetings?
- ☐ For the next week, notice the times when you get interrupted and have to shift from one task to another. What does this do to your productivity?

☐ Notice what the organization's leaders talk the most about: winning products, speed, cost, quality, or some combination. What does that say about your organization's mastery of innovation?

THE HISTORY OF LEAN THINKING

"Lean" is not an acronym or a synonym for "cut the fat." It is the word that MIT graduate student John Krafcik first used in 1988 to denote a few automotive companies that had achieved outstanding results year after year as documented in MIT's International Motor Vehicle Research Project. In 1990, the project's leaders, James Womack and Daniel T. Jones, published their results in *The Machine That Changed the World* and "Lean" became a management buzzword—but one with extraordinary sticking power. Twenty-two years later, it is hard to find a U.S. manufacturing organization that does not claim to be Lean.

LEAN TOOLS

In the early 1990s, "Lean Manufacturing" described a set of manufacturing practices gleaned from studies of the Toyota Production System, especially the methods that Taichi Ohno pioneered in the 1950s and spent the rest of his career refining. The Lean Manufacturing toolkit included concepts like work cells, just-in-time, and one-piece flow. Throughout the 1990s, most Lean Manufacturing programs focused on the tools without looking deeper.

These practices dramatically improved manufacturing performance, but they didn't always work and the improvements didn't always stick. When Lean tools moved off the factory floor into creative areas of the business, they didn't work well at all. Lean Thinkers had to look deeper to understand why Toyota had such a long track record of profitable growth.

LEAN CULTURE

Researchers like Jeffrey Liker and Jim Womack kept digging, and they found that Toyota's management system was the real secret. Toyota applied this philosophy across the entire business, not just on the manufacturing floor. Today, we have Lean Office, Lean Logistics, Lean Accounting, Lean Supply Chain, and Lean Product Development—all wrapped up in the Lean enterprise. The management system was the key to pull it all together, and culture change was the rallying cry to create a Lean Enterprise.

Yet that wasn't enough either. First, Toyota grew too fast in the early 2000s and stumbled—with aggressive cost reductions that hurt the customer experience and major recalls that tarnished its reputation for high quality. Second, cultural differences didn't fully explain why some companies were able to make Lean stick and then spread it beyond manufacturing. Third, "culture" became an excuse for not doing anything at all with Lean methods. Yet the emphasis on culture came from the companies where Lean failed—not where Lean succeeded. What was different about them?

LEAN PROBLEM SOLVING

Toyota's challenges in the 2000s helped by pointing out what went wrong: In all the emphasis on cost reduction, global expansion, and market share growth, the company forgot to make sure that everyone in the organization solved problems systematically. At the same time, when we look at the companies, including those in this book, that have made Lean stick over a long time, we see that it's their ability to solve problems systematically that has kept them going. Today, we recognize that systematic problem solving to maximize value and minimize waste is the core of Lean Thinking.

2

Value and Waste in Product Development

Jim Womack defined **value** entirely from the customer's perspective: "The right product to the right customer at the right price and at the right time." A **product** is anything a company delivers to customers: tangible products, software, and services all must deliver value. They all go through a **product development process** (PDP) that transforms them from an idea into something that a customer can purchase and use, as well as operational processes to produce and deliver them. In theory, if a product delivers sufficient customer value relative to its competitors, it will be a successful product.

Since this is not always true, most organizations expand the definition of value to include the **business value**—the profit and competitive advantage—that the company gains through delivering the product. This is ultimately the criterion that will determine whether or not the product is a success. All new product ideas need a strong **business case:** the rationale that shows the customer and business value that the new product will deliver, and the justification for investing time, energy, and money into developing the specific product.

VALUE-CREATING ACTIVITIES AND WASTE

Value-creating activities are those steps that must be taken for the product to reach the customer. On a manufacturing floor, we can easily distinguish value-creating activities because they transform materials into products in some tangible way. All the other activities, including many things that seem essential, are **waste:** defects, scrap, excess motion, transportation, storage, inspection, and all management activities. In product development, any activity that builds customer or technical knowledge, or uses knowledge to design the product, is value creation.

Lean distinguishes between unnecessary waste and necessary waste. Most people see **unnecessary waste:** defects, excess motion, and scrap. It's obvious that removing these from the system will make the system better. **Necessary waste** is all the non-value-creating work we do in order to keep the system working in its current state. In product development, unnecessary waste looks like the bugs that cause rework late in development. Necessary waste includes project management activities, most documentation, verification testing, and status reports.

Many of the big performance gains we see from Lean Manufacturing arise from reducing the level of necessary waste: cutting inventory with pull systems, reducing transportation with better layouts, shortening changeover times so that we can run smaller batch sizes economically, and using better management methods that refocus managers' efforts on supporting the people who do value-creating work rather than controlling them. In product development, reducing the burden of documentation, project management overhead, and other necessary waste gives product developers more time to innovate.

To make things even more challenging, we may choose to add necessary waste to one part of a system to improve the health of the whole system. For example, we may add an extra inspection step right after a processing step that tends to generate defects in order to detect and then eventually eliminate the defects from that processing step. We may need that inspection to generate the data to help us understand the root causes of the problem so that we can fix it permanently, and to avoid wasting work on defective parts. Once we have eliminated the source of the defects, we can remove the extra inspection.

In product development, we may do more frequent planning sessions early to reduce the waste of design changes late in development.

Value streams are sequences of value-creating activities, necessary waste, and unnecessary waste. We use "value stream" to replace the term "process" to highlight the importance of understanding how value flows through the value-creating activities, removing unnecessary waste and ensuring that all necessary waste truly supports the delivery of maximum value.

LEARNING TO SEE WASTE IN PRODUCT DEVELOPMENT

On a manufacturing floor, waste is easy to see once you know what you're looking for. Taichi Ohno, the developer of the Toyota Production System, defined seven wastes in manufacturing: excess inventory, extra steps, extra transportation, waiting, defects, excess motion, and overproduction. You can see these things just by walking a manufacturing floor.

It's harder to see the waste in product development because the "product" of new product development is knowledge: knowledge about customers and knowledge about technologies and process capabilities integrated into specific knowledge about how to make a product—the product design. Some people have gone to great lengths to create analogies for Ohno's seven wastes in product development, but that seems to me like an unnecessary stretch. We have plenty of waste of our own, once we know what to look for.

Since knowledge is the value created in product development, it tends to be hidden in the IT systems and tools we use to create and store our knowledge, as well as within our seasoned engineers' minds. The tangible things we produce in product development—all the drawings, prototypes, compiled code bases, and test reports—are merely artifacts for capturing knowledge. They are only valuable to the extent that they faithfully capture knowledge. It does no good to measure whether or not a drawing is completed if one has no way to know whether or not the drawing adequately captures all the information necessary to deliver the part, and whether or not the part works in the context of the entire system.

COMMON WASTES IN PRODUCT DEVELOPMENT

Here are the common forms of product development waste that the case study companies directly attacked in their Lean Product Development programs:

- **Design loopbacks:** This is the most obvious source of waste in product development. A product gets almost all of the way to the end; the team thinks it's about ready to ship and then discovers something that sets them back weeks or even months. By the time they find the problem, fixing it requires a lot of expensive redesign and retesting.

- **Reinvention:** Reinvention is the need to redesign or rework something because previous solutions to a problem are not accessible to the problem solver or not generalized enough to be reusable. The waste of reinvention consumes resources that would be put to better use on innovation; it leads to part proliferation, and it increases the probability of late design changes.

- **Unproductive meetings:** Any meeting that does not have a clear purpose or that results in no clear decisions or actions is waste. This includes all of the meetings we hold just to communicate status.

- **Insufficient customer empathy:** We cannot deliver customer value if we don't know what customer value is. The most wasteful thing a product development organization can do is to deliver the wrong product.

- **Excess requirements and specifications:** Excess requirements and specifications create waste in three ways: We develop things the customer does not want, we build products to rigid specifications that rob us of the ability to maximize value as our knowledge increases and we have to maintain the extra product complexity throughout the life of the product.

- **Excess project management overhead:** Project management is necessary waste. Product development is too complex to do without some way to track schedules and budgets. At the same time, all the effort expended on project management contributes nothing to customer value and may in fact make it harder for developers to contribute value.

- **Overloaded resources:** If product developers have too many projects and do not have a prioritized list of projects to work from, then senior product development managers have delegated responsibility for making strategic decisions to the people least equipped to make those decisions. The overload slows product development down and ultimately leads to fewer new products—the opposite of what everyone intended.

VALUE AND WASTE IN PRODUCT DEVELOPMENT

All of this is much harder to see in product development, which does not proceed in a linear fashion from raw materials to finished product. The value of product development is the organizational knowledge we develop so that we can produce and deliver a product. The knowledge is embedded in a long list of deliverables that help us transfer this knowledge to the people who need it: prototypes, drawings, assembly instructions, test results, tooling specifications, etc. We can easily see the deliverables but the process of creating them is almost completely invisible in most organizations.

Since knowledge is the value that flows in product development, we can find the value-creating activities if we look for

- The activities that build knowledge about our customers: their needs, their behaviors, and their environments.
- The activities that build knowledge about our product technology: fundamental science, design alternatives, supplier and manufacturing capabilities.
- The activities that integrate customer and technical knowledge into products that we can produce and our customers want to buy.

Everything else is waste.

Unnecessary waste in product development is frustrating and visible. It's hard to hide missed communications, mistakes that don't get caught until they get built into expensive prototypes, unproductive meetings that don't lead to clear decisions and actions, waiting due to overloaded test resources or inadequate equipment, and the need to reinvent something because a previous solution cannot be found or is not reusable. We can go faster by simply eliminating these unnecessary wastes, but Lean Product Development companies don't stop there.

As with Lean Manufacturing, a lot of the big productivity gains come when we replace our current "necessary waste" with better methods that require less time, energy, and money. We replace complex specifications documents with a series of smaller documents that are easier to write and update. We replace sophisticated project management with tools that allow teams to manage more of their own work flow. We replace major stage gate reviews that require weeks of preparation with more frequent, less formal opportunities to review progress.

THE FOUR VALUE STREAMS OF LEAN PRODUCT DEVELOPMENT

To make things even more interesting, product developers have four value streams to optimize if they want to master innovation (Figure 2.1): the customer value stream, the knowledge creation value stream, the product design and test value stream, and the production value stream.

The Customer Value Stream

Product developers must understand what constitutes customer value and how to deliver it. This sounds simple, but most companies have multiple customers with conflicting needs: distributors, resellers, recommenders, purchasers, and end users. For example, a medical device company's customers include doctors, patients, nurses, insurance

FIGURE 2.1
The four value streams of product development.

companies, and/or national health services. Insurance companies and national health services want to hold down costs. Patients want to be free from pain as soon as possible and need devices they can incorporate into their daily routines. Doctors want reliable treatment outcomes. Nurses need to be able to use the device in a hectic hospital setting without disrupting the flow of their work.

Value in this value stream consists of the function that customers want to realize when they purchase a product. This is not always obvious: Most people don't buy computers to "compute" anything. They buy computers to connect with the online world, to do their work, to get better grades, or to express their creativity. Waste in any of these customer value streams presents an opportunity to deliver a product that is more compelling than competitors' offerings. Waste often shows up as customer "dissatisfiers." Products that take too long to set up, are too hard to use, eat up too much battery power, or break down too often generate waste for customers.

Innovations that decrease cost, improve quality, and increase ease of use increase customer value. Breakthrough products often arise from the ability to recognize and remove waste that's so prevalent that it's hard to see: Digital cameras and Facebook eliminate the need for purchasing, storing, installing, and processing film just so that we can share our family pictures.

Lean Product Development emphasizes building deep customer knowledge through activities that help us develop customer empathy: the ability to sense customers' stated and unstated needs when they are in their natural environments so that we can make decisions that maximize value for the customers. Lean Product Development leaders understand that this is too vital to rely upon a single function to gather and interpret this information: Sales and marketing staff, senior technologists, designers, and engineers all benefit from direct customer experience.

The Knowledge Creation Value Stream

The knowledge creation value stream is the process of building, capturing, and sharing technical and customer knowledge. Technical knowledge includes things like manufacturing capabilities, algorithms, materials properties, and simulation methods. Customer knowledge is the understanding of what customers value, what they experience as waste, and how their behavior and environment impact their ability to use the product to get the things they value.

Value in this value stream consists of the ability to create and capture knowledge rapidly and efficiently that can be shared across many products. This value stream is present inside every organization but it was completely invisible until Ikujiro Nonaka of Hitotsubashi University in Tokyo released his research into organizational knowledge creation. His work, documented in *The Knowledge Creating Company* in 1995, demonstrated that the companies that understood the process of knowledge creation had the ability to be faster, more innovative, and more predictably successful.

The true benefits from the knowledge creation value stream appear when the organization has the ability to capitalize on its knowledge to deliver innovative products that meet customers' needs better than anything they would have expected. Lean Product Development has an entire toolkit devoted to creating, capturing, and sharing reusable knowledge—knowledge that can be leveraged from one product to another to deliver unique customer value, eliminate reinvention, and reduce technical risk:

- Explicitly allocate resources to create reusable knowledge in the form of studies to understand the fundamental science behind the product technology. This knowledge is broadly applicable to reduce trial and error during design and a significant source of competitive advantage, since it is not easily copied. It gives product developers the ability to understand the limits of their current design and to identify opportunities for innovative products where there are overlaps between product technology and customer needs that are not represented in products today.
- Build an infrastructure for sharing knowledge that facilitates knowledge reuse. Simple systems work better than complex systems, and people are more likely to reuse knowledge from trusted sources that is generalized and actionable.
- Make it easier to reuse knowledge than it is to create something new: Part libraries, design templates, and simulation models can all embed the organization's best technical knowledge so that the path of least resistance is to use the organization's knowledge as much as possible.

The ability to capitalize on an organization's knowledge supercharges a team's ability to innovate by helping them see the areas of opportunity where innovation will be the most valuable, and by ensuring that they don't have to waste a single brain cell on anything routine.

The Product Design and Test Value Stream

This is the value stream that integrates knowledge into product designs and then verifies that the products work as expected. It is the value stream most of us think of when we describe our product development process (PDP). Value in this value stream consists of the ability to rapidly convert generalized knowledge into product-specific knowledge that operations and delivery partners can use to produce a product that delivers good customer value at a low cost with high reliability.

Almost all of the practices embedded in an organization's PDP are part of this value stream. Stage gate life cycles, co-development, and product development portfolio management are all part of the product design and test value stream. In organizations that are not aware of the importance of the knowledge creation value stream, this may be all there is to their PDP. They entirely miss the ability to create, capture, and share knowledge outside a product development program.

To make things worse, a lot of conventional wisdom about how to optimize these processes slows them down. Many executives and engineering managers believe that an overloaded, multitasking engineer is a more productive engineer. Yet overloaded engineers generate defects and take shortcuts that create rework that is often not discovered until late in development when fixes are expensive. Multitasking is not conducive to knowledge sharing and reuse because these conversations require focused attention. Standard phase gate processes incorporate rigidity into a system that requires flexibility.

Lean Product Development builds this value stream into a network of adaptable systems, processes, and tools that maximize value and eliminate waste in an environment of complexity and uncertainty:

- Do the knowledge creation work up front to minimize technical and market risk so that this part of the life cycle can proceed with a minimum of late surprises.
- Use checklists and design guidelines to ensure that the organization's best available knowledge is accessible to product developers throughout the organization.
- Eliminate waste in the transactional "microprocesses" that comprise this value stream. Processes for qualifying new suppliers, ordering tools, performing standard tests, passing regulatory compliance, and even logging project files in and out of systems are all opportunities

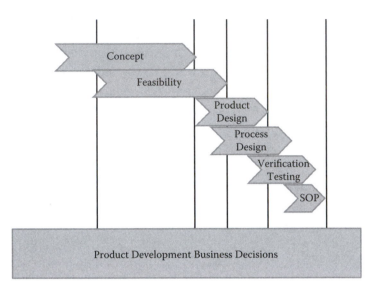

FIGURE 2.2
A Lean product development process.

> to save time by eliminating the wastes of waiting, overprocessing, inspection, rework, and excess inventory.
>
> - Replace rigid stage gate processes with frameworks that are more scalable and adaptable to the needs of specific product teams (Figure 2.2).

This powerful combination simultaneously accelerates product development, frees up capacity, improves quality, and lowers cost.

The Production Value Stream

The final value stream is the one that impacts the organization the most. The production value stream is the process of converting raw materials into finished goods, delivering those goods to customers, and then supporting the products throughout their life cycle. For companies that produce a tangible product, this is the most visible value stream. One can walk the manufacturing floor to see how the product comes together. For manufacturing and other operations partners, we maximize value by improving our ability to make and deliver products as quickly as possible at low cost and high quality. We seek to reduce the time it takes to convert raw materials into a new product, to increase a plant's capacity to build products, and to reduce costs and eliminate defects.

The most common source of product redesign is an unanticipated problem that arises the first time someone attempts to build a new product using standard manufacturing processes. Even the best companies always have a few of these, but if they are rampant, they can delay a product by years.

Just as product developers need deep customer knowledge to maximize the customer value stream, they need deep understanding of their company's manufacturing capabilities. In many organizations, the manufacturing process is the domain of specialized manufacturing engineers who turn product designs into process and tool designs. These people often do not see a new product until it is far down the design path and decisions are hard to change. If a product development team receives no input from manufacturing until this late, the product is almost guaranteed to be late. At the same time, if manufacturing engineers have veto power over designs too early in the process, they have the potential to shut down innovation. It will take some experimentation and learning to find the right balance.

Lean product development addresses this in three ways:

- Treat manufacturing capability as part of the knowledge creation value stream alongside technical and customer knowledge, with practices to support knowledge creation, capture, and sharing.
- Identify the causes of late design changes that stem from manufacturability issues and capture the lessons learned into design checklists that developers can use to prevent these problems from happening again.
- Engage advanced manufacturing engineers early in the process, but give them responsibility for identifying risks—not blocking innovative ideas you just don't know how to make yet. This role should include investigating manufacturing capability improvements and new methods as well as assisting teams with making design decisions that make the best use of existing manufacturing capability.

This concept applies in service organizations as well. Service delivery processes also have capabilities to understand, known problems to avoid, limitations to overcome, and opportunities to exploit.

Discussion Questions

- Which of the wastes described in this chapter are familiar to you?
- How Lean is your PDP? Specifically, if you use a phase gate process, how flexible are the gates and is it possible to overlap the phases when it makes sense?
- How well do you understand your plant's manufacturing capabilities?

Next Actions

- ☐ Build some customer knowledge: Visit a place where a customer buys or uses your product and observe how customers interact with it. What do you see?
- ☐ Eliminate the waste of unproductive meetings: Don't hold a meeting unless there is a decision to make or an action to take, send out an agenda in advance, keep laptops closed during meetings, and find other ways to report status information.
- ☐ If you write documentation, talk to one of your recipients to see if the format can be streamlined so that it's easier for you to write and easier for others to read.

EXEMPLARS OF LEAN IN PRODUCT DEVELOPMENT

Although the International Motor Vehicle Project identified several companies that fit the "Lean" profile, only Toyota was open enough to share its methods with the world. As a result, "Lean Manufacturing" is equivalent to the Toyota Production System. In the last 20 years, dozens of books have focused on Toyota's management systems.

Toyota's reputation in product development circles is mixed. While Toyotas have high quality, BMWs, Mercedes, Volvos, and Volkswagens have a better reputation for innovation. Toyota is not included on the three most recent lists of most innovative companies from *Fast Company,* MIT's *Technology Review,* or *Forbes Magazine.*

Meanwhile, other companies have built strong track records of innovation using practices that maximize value and minimize waste in product development. Here are five public companies that exemplify Lean Product Development, even if they don't use the word "Lean" themselves:

- **Apple:** Apple's products are models of simplicity, elegance, and maximum customer value. Apple's ability to understand and maximize customer value has delivered powerful results. The iPod was not just a music player—it was an entirely new ecosystem that solved the problem of how to distribute music online while protecting royalties for artists and record companies. The iPhone dominated the market for smart phones within two years of its release, and the iPad invented the tablet product category.
- **Google:** Google has developed unique methods for beta-testing new ideas with customers and tracking online behavior to understand how well these concepts have been received. Its entire product architecture and systems allow for rapid development, testing, and deployment of new ideas without any risk to core products. They use these tools to build customer and technical knowledge that they integrate into new products.
- **Facebook:** Facebook eliminated waste in an Internet user's value stream for connecting with friends, sharing photos, and spreading news within social networks. In the process, the company

developed an advertising platform and marketing engine that help companies reach the specific users most likely to want their products.

- **Amazon:** Amazon's "product" is the e-commerce platform that the company uses to sell its own products and to facilitate online sales from other merchants, even those who compete with Amazon's own core business. Amazon pioneered such innovations as customer reviews, a powerful recommendation engine, and "one-click" ordering that eliminate waste in the online shopper's value stream. The company's willingness to extend this platform to other merchants has helped it to dominate the market by eliminating the waste of reinvention for online sellers.

- **Starbucks:** This is the company that taught people to pay more than $3 for a cup of coffee by educating them about what good coffee tastes like. The company's retail stores give it a natural channel for testing out new ideas among a passionate customer community. Its willingness to challenge assumptions has led to innovations like Via, the world's first gourmet instant coffee. Its ability to surface problems and admit mistakes helped it recover its product quality when rapid expansion led to lower standards. While the company may not say much about Lean Product Development, its actions demonstrate the power of systematic problem solving in an innovation-driven business.

3

The Lean Product Development Benchmarking Study

The companies who provided stories for this book have mastered innovation with Lean Product Development. They have demonstrated that a company can reduce time to market by more than half, triple R & D capacity, and lower costs using Lean Product Development methods—and that the company can keep getting better.

What about the long-term results? The companies featured here have five years of experience with Lean Product Development, on average. As of April 2012, all of the Lean Product Development practices that you will find in this book are still in use within these companies. All of them have seen their efforts bear fruit—some of them for many years now. For some of these companies, Lean has just become the way that things get done, and no one can imagine what it would be like to do product development in a different way.

WHERE DID THESE COMPANIES COME FROM?

This book is the final product of the Lean Product Development Benchmarking Study that I launched in 2010, although it came out quite differently than I had imagined it would. The study set out to answer these three questions:

- What does "Lean Product Development" mean to the companies that use it?

- When people say that they use Lean Product Development, what are they actually doing?
- What results do they see?

I originally planned to conduct an online survey and then follow up the survey with additional interviews. The survey did not attract enough respondents to be statistically significant, but almost all of the respondents invited me to learn more about them. Their survey responses surprised me. Many of them had longer histories with Lean Product Development than I had expected.

I spent most of 2011 traveling from company to company, interviewing Lean Product Developers and observing their practices in action. I visited as many of these companies as possible in person. Then I conducted interviews by phone for the rest. I also reviewed presentations the sponsors had delivered at conferences, papers they had published in academic journals, and the internal documentation that supported their Lean Product Development practices. By the time my travels had come to an end, I had filled several thick three-ring binders with handwritten notes and supporting documents.

In all, I interviewed 63 companies in seven countries and a wide variety of industries. Twelve of the companies that I visited had stories that were compelling enough that I decided to devote an entire chapter to each. Another set had achieved significant results with a specific practice or tool. They became the capsule case studies at the end of the main case study chapters.

Not every company I visited ended up in this book, and I did not visit every company that invited me. Some companies experienced significant changes, sometimes proving that their implementation of Lean Product Development did not sustain itself. Other companies did not meet the high standards that the case study companies set for them, their stories were too similar to those of another company that I had already decided to include, or they felt that they did not want to share the details of their work with the entire product development community.

A DIVERSE SET OF COMPANIES

The primary criterion I used to determine whether or not to include a company in this study was the company's demonstrated results with Lean

Product Development. The case study sponsor needed to demonstrate that all of the effort it took to bring Lean Product Development inside the company had paid off. I needed visible results.

From among the Lean Product Development organizations that had achieved significant results, I intentionally chose to visit companies that varied along these four dimensions:

- Size: Annual revenue ranges from $10 million to over $250 billion per year.
- Industry: The companies represent a range of high-tech to low-tech industries, emerging versus mature markets, and narrow versus broad product diversity (Figure 3.1).
- Organizational structure: Some of these companies are large, publicly traded firms facing relentless pressure to deliver quarterly results. Others are privately held firms whose owners have a long-term perspective on the business.
- Geography: Some have a small geographic footprint; others have sites located all over the world. I chose to focus on companies based in North America and in Western Europe because those are the two regions where Lean Product Development has achieved critical mass, with local and regional Lean Product Development net-

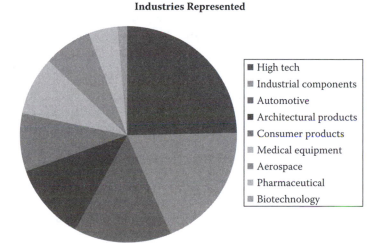

Industries Represented

- High tech
- Industrial components
- Automotive
- Architectural products
- Consumer products
- Medical equipment
- Aerospace
- Pharmaceutical
- Biotechnology

FIGURE 3.1
Industries represented in the LPD Benchmarking Study.

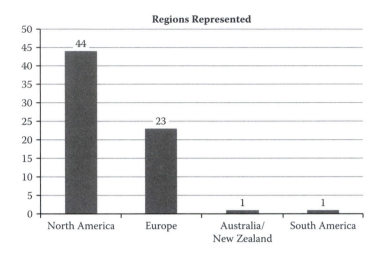

FIGURE 3.2
Regions represented in the LPD Benchmarking Study.

works, university–industry partnerships, and regular conferences and public training events (Figure 3.2). I interviewed one company each from Brazil and New Zealand by telephone.

When product development leaders are in the midst of deciding whether and how to do Lean Product Development, it helps to know that companies like theirs have used Lean Product Development successfully. It was important to make sure that I covered as much of the ground as possible in the time I had.

Although I could have packed this book with my current and former clients, only three of the case studies come directly from my own consulting work (Vaisala, Buckeye Technologies, and Playworld Systems). This was a conscious choice: I decided to reach beyond my own client base to find other companies who had approached Lean Product Development from different angles. The investment in time and energy would only be worth it to me if I learned as much as my readers, and that was only possible if I cast my net as broadly as possible.

"What Does Lean Product Development Mean to You?"

Each of the companies in this book has a different view of Lean Product Development. Some of them have chosen to focus on waste elimination and process optimization. Others use visual management as a starting point to give teams their first experiences with Lean practices. A few have embraced Allen Ward's vision of Lean Product Development that is grounded in the principles of the Toyota Product Development System, as he understood it. Others have adapted Toyota's product development practices to their own. Some synthesized Lean Thinking with Agile Development to revolutionize their product development process. Others took a more incremental approach to change.

The key takeaway is that no one—no consultant, no author, not even Toyota itself—has a comprehensive view of Lean Product Development as it expresses itself in industry today. Most of the companies in this book consulted several different experts, read a collection of books, and attended trainings from different service providers. It is only by looking at what each of these companies has done that one can build a complete picture of what a Lean Product Development organization is capable of doing.

Only two of the companies in this book, Ford Motor Company and Scania, are in the same industry as Toyota. Only one, Visteon, is a Toyota supplier. For everyone else in this book, the first step with Lean Product Development was to decide whether and how these concepts applied to them. For products such as seating systems that rely heavily on mechanical engineering with well-known materials, the analogies were easy to find. For Novo Nordisk, a pharmaceutical company, or Buckeye Technologies, a specialty fiber company, the standard methods required a lot of adaptation.

At first, any individual or team can begin simply to experiment with the practices of Lean Product Development, especially the practice of surfacing problems and then fixing them permanently. At some point, usually after a few early experiments have come through, the time comes when a product development group needs to answer the questions: "What does Lean Product Development mean for us? If we were a Lean Product Development organization, how would we be better off?"

At the same time, the process of figuring out what Lean Product Development means is an important step in a Lean Transformation, and it is the kind of thing that no external person or group can do. Only the people on the ground—the people who are closest to the problems—are the ones who understand which concepts have the most resonance, and which words will create the best connections between the problems that people see in front of them and the new behaviors they will be asked to adopt.

GO-AND-SEE

Toyota is not always the best model for Lean product developers, yet there is one aspect of Toyota's management system that every product developer should know and use: *genchi genbutsu* or "go-and-see."

Go-and-see is the practice of going to the "real place" where things happen and seeing the situation firsthand. If you need to solve a problem at a customer site, then you need to understand the problem at the customer's site. Usually, this means you need to go-and-see the problem for yourself. No descriptions, pictures, or even video will convey the wealth of knowledge that we gain by going to the real place ourselves. Our human senses have the ability to take in much more from the environment than a camera, especially those things that the people who live in the environment no longer notice. We can talk to the people who are there to learn more about the problem and how it impacts them. We can look beyond the obvious problem to find root causes.

In *The Knowledge Creating Company,* Nonaka and Takeuchi describe the difference between tacit knowledge and explicit knowledge (see the figure following this section). Anything that someone can send you via e-mail is explicit knowledge, which can only capture a small percentage of the knowledge that an experienced person has developed. Tacit knowledge is the stuff that's hard to write down, and the only way to get it is from direct experience. When we write down something we learned through experience, we externalize it. We can turn explicit knowledge into tacit knowledge by internalizing it: working with it and gaining experience with it ourselves.

When we go to the real place, we build tacit knowledge as well as explicit knowledge. When we go-and-see a problem in its own environment, we also naturally encounter the people who are closest to the problem, and we have the opportunity to help them externalize their tacit knowledge by asking questions and observing how they interact with the problem.

You can structure a go-and-see visit with interviews, but it's important to allow unstructured time to share a meal, wander the halls, and see what you observe just from being in the same environment.

You might notice something—the temperature or humidity level, a machine that's not set properly, or an uneven floor—that the people in the environment no longer notice.

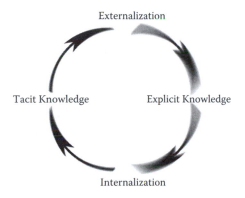

Tacit and explicit knowledge.

Although many of the definitions of Lean Product Development resemble each other so much that one could accuse the companies of reinvention, the process of committing the words and images to paper was the most important part. When the members of a group define Lean Product Development for themselves, they own the definition—and therefore responsibility for its success.

The answer to this question determines where the teams will focus. For each of the companies represented in this book, the answer was different. I have seen few successful Lean Product Development implementations that arrived at the same answer. The right answer is the one that speaks to an organization's greatest hopes and deepest fears.

"What Results Have You Seen?"

Lean Product Development is too difficult to do simply because it seems like a good idea. The companies featured in this book had some compelling need, some important problem that needed to be solved. Lean Product Development had to demonstrate its worth by delivering results that mattered.

Before answering what Lean Product Development means, the teams needed to understand what it would do for them—how the results would make a difference. They needed to know that the investment in time and energy would deliver the results that the company needed. The mastery of innovation requires not just knowing what to do, but knowing why it works, and what the expected results will be.

The companies represented in this book have almost universally decreased time to market, sometimes dramatically. When product development is fast enough to synchronize with the market need for new products, the capacity gets reinvested into delivering more new products per year. Some of the companies also achieved gains in quality, cost, or customer value.

"When You Say That You Do Lean Product Development, What Do You Actually Do?"

As diverse as these companies and their paths have been, there are some common threads that extend across all of the case studies:

Systematic problem solving: Nearly all of these companies have adopted some form of systematic problem solving that supports closed learning cycles. They use classic PDCA, LAMDA, or some other learning cycle. The method chosen is much less important than the decision to choose one method that everyone will use. Without a method to surface problems and then develop effective countermeasures, waste is difficult to see and nearly impossible to eliminate. Without a common method, people waste time arguing about semantics instead of solving the problems at hand.

Visualization to surface problems and share knowledge: The Lean Product Development organization consciously makes its knowledge visible and works to surface problems. At Irwin Seating, this takes the form of an obeya room that consolidates all of the information in one place. At Philips Electronics in Drachten, a visual project management system keeps the most important issues right in front of the product development teams. Visteon has taken a visual approach to managing the organization's key knowledge and deliverables.

Pilot teams followed by knowledge sharing: Almost all of these companies began Lean Product Development with a pilot project and, at large companies like Scania, pilots are still the means for moving Lean Product Development into new organizations. Once a new practice or tool has been tested, it can be shared with other teams. This is not the standardization of a manufacturing floor—knowledge sharing still provides lots of room for freedom of motion.

WHAT SURPRISED ME

As I visited the companies and began compiling the notes, a few things stood out.

SBCE

It was a surprise to me that set-based concurrent engineering (SBCE) received few mentions in the companies I visited. This is the engineering method that Allen Ward developed theoretically and then found inside Toyota in the 1990s. After that, Michael Kennedy published two books describing the practice in more depth.

I found a few examples of convergence, but none of SBCE as envisioned by Allen Ward and Michael Kennedy. I saw a lot of interest in the topic and a few pilots, but no sustainable examples among all the companies I talked with. I suspect that this is because SBCE is complex and difficult to master and, in most product development organizations, other Lean practices get results faster. It's possible that there are companies using SBCE who did not know about the study or chose not to participate.

Value Stream Maps

Value stream mapping is a Lean Operations tool for visualizing a value stream. It highlights the value-creating activities, unnecessary waste, delays, and rework loops. Some Lean Product Development experts use this tool extensively and others hardly use it at all. In all cases, it requires adaptation to map product development processes accurately.

I expected to find that value stream maps had been either ignored, or tried and then abandoned. Instead, I found that many of the companies had adapted value stream mapping so that it worked for them: It highlighted the wastes and barriers to flow that were most important for that organization. A Lean Operations expert would hardly recognize some of the results, yet the Lean Product Development program teams had been able to eliminate a lot of waste and dramatically improve the flow of work through product development. As a result, I've spent more time myself in the past year doing value stream maps or knowledge flow maps with my own clients, and I've seen good results.

Virtual Visual Planning

Visual planning is a Lean tool for making project plans and work flows more visible at the team level, and brings problems to the surface. It increases ownership for the team's plans. For a team in the same office, a visual project plan can consist of Post-it® notes placed on a gridded whiteboard that represents a time line. Rows represent people or subteams and columns depict time slices. Sticky notes record activities to be placed in the cell that represents the intersection of the activity owner and the time slice when the activity will be done.

I witnessed numerous experiments to spread the benefits of visual project planning to teams that were not located in the same office. Groups tried projecting onto interactive whiteboards, using synched LCD screens that showed the same project plan at several sites simultaneously, and a wide variety of webcam setups to display visual plans across different sites. None of these countermeasures are working well—yet. As LCD and touch screen technology continues to improve, these experiments will lead the way toward a real solution.

SUGGESTIONS FOR USING THE CASE STUDIES

These companies have achieved dramatic results: faster time to market, better market coverage, higher quality, and lower costs. Give this book to the people in your organization who care about these results. Mark the case studies that show how a company solved the most important problems that you face.

These case studies will not provide enough detail for you to learn how to use the practices they describe just from reading this book. For that, I would have had to write a book on each case study. Instead, I encourage you to read these case studies to spark ideas and to give you inspiration to learn more about Lean Product Development.

If you want to learn more about how to use the practices mentioned in this book, you can look for resources on the Lean Product Development Resource Center website (http://lpdrc.com). There you will find examples, templates, and knowledge briefs that describe the specific practices in more depth than I can do here.

Three of the case studies in this book mention book study groups as one of the first things that they did. This has proven to be a good way to begin building core knowledge about Lean Product Development. Appendix 2 shares some best practices for organizing a book study group inside your company.

Discussion Questions

- What does Lean product development mean to you?
- Which companies in this book are most similar to yours? How can you learn from them?
- What systematic problem solving methods do you already use inside your company?

Next Actions

- ☐ Send out an e-mail to invite people to join you in a book study group.
- ☐ Use your company's systematic problem solving method to eliminate a source of waste you identified in Chapter 2. If you don't have one, use LAMDA.
- ☐ Sign up for a membership at the Lean Product Development Resource Center (http://lpdrc.com) and spend some time exploring what you find there.

Section II

The Pioneers of Lean Product Development

4

DJO Global: The Fundamentals of Lean Product Development

When DJO Global (DJO) began to bring Lean Thinking into its R & D labs in 2003, Lean Product Development was in its infancy. There was not much in the way of external examples to guide them. The books that laid the theoretical framework for Lean Product Development had not yet been published, and Lean Product Developers still suffered from the inappropriate use of Lean Manufacturing tools in product development processes. DJO's engineers would need to build their own model because there was no model to follow.

DJO makes a variety of products that support knees, shoulders, and other joints during recovery from injury or surgery. When Lean Product Development got underway, the R & D organization was based entirely in San Diego, with manufacturing sites there and in Mexico. Even though the team had all the advantages of small size and a single site, they still had a lot of waste and a lot of opportunities to maximize value. Rich Gildersleeve, Chief Technology Officer, recalls, "When we started, we could only release a handful of products per year, and they took too long to get to market. That was not enough to support DJO's growth. Naturally, we looked to Lean to help us get better."

DJO's leadership team had already seen the value of Lean in operations when they began applying Lean to product development more than 10 years ago. The COO at the time, Luke Faulstick, strongly encouraged Rich and his team to see if Lean could help them eliminate the barriers that kept DJO's best ideas from reaching the market.

ABOUT DJO GLOBAL

DJO Global is a $1 billion, 5,200 employee company headquartered in Vista, California, with major development sites in Texas, North Carolina, and Switzerland. DJO is a leader in orthopedic technologies used for rehabilitation, pain management, physical therapy, and surgical reconstruction; brands include Donjoy, Empi, Chattanooga, CMF, Compex, DJO Surgical, ETI, Bell-Horn, and Procare. The company has served as a leader in the Lean community, with key leadership positions in the Association for Manufacturing Excellence, and the Lean Product & Process Development Exchange, Inc. Their corporate website is http://www.djo.com.

LEAN PRODUCT DEVELOPMENT AT DJO

DJO stuck to two fundamentals of Lean Thinking: What is value and how can we maximize it? What is waste and how can we eliminate it? Along the way, the R & D team developed some innovative countermeasures to the common wastes in product development. DJO's experiences on the leading edge of Lean Product Development bring value—and waste—into sharp relief.

DJO has seen that a lot of the big productivity gains come when "necessary waste"—documentation, project management, and routine testing—is replaced with better methods that require less time, energy, and money. Complex specifications documents have been replaced with a series of smaller documents that are easier to write and update. The company uses simple project management tools that allow teams to manage more of their own work flow. It has replaced major stage gate reviews that require weeks of preparation with more frequent opportunities to review progress.

Rich asked the engineers to track—anonymously—the time they spent on value-added activities versus the time spent in meetings, updating reports, and other non-value-added work. The company found that during the development phase, its engineers spent 50% of their time adding value to the product—defined as "any task that directly deepens or transfers useful knowledge to the final product." The other half mostly consisted of "mandated waste" imposed by the current state of the system. During the "fuzzy front end," the numbers were much worse: Only 10% of time was spent adding value.

Rich worked diligently over a number of years to instill a culture of continuous improvement inside DJO's R & D. He walked the talk himself by participating in kaizen blitz events to eliminate bureaucracy in the product development process. *Kaizen* is a Japanese term meaning "improvement" and kaizen events are workshops specifically designed to help a team improve a specific area of the business, usually by identifying and eliminating waste. For example, a kaizen blitz in 2008 to simplify the design of a battery housing assembly eliminated $50,000 of monthly costs in two days.

Jeff Culhane, Vice President of Surgical R & D, led a four-day blitz to reduce the number of approvals needed for start of production (SOP) significantly. His team developed the SKU A3 to serve as the single source of key information about a product. This single-sided 11 × 17 report summarizes the project status, user needs, targets and requirements, risks, and verification plans for a product. The documents that feed this A3 were also streamlined and slimmed down. This change reduced the number of forms required from 66 to 28, a 58% reduction in documentation. The number of signatures required dropped from 117 to 46, a 61% improvement.

Along the way, Rich learned that sustainable change needs team involvement. He has enlisted R & D's partner organizations to help his teams find ways to speed up projects by reducing non-value-added activities and deliverables. The experiments they have conducted in cross-functional teams have a much higher rate of sustainability than changes that one person or a small team tried to do alone.

PROTOSTORMING

Inspired by Allen Ward's writings on SBCE and IDEO's description of their rapid prototyping processes, DJO developed protostorming. Protostorming jump-starts a product development program with a focused, cross-functional team effort to develop an innovative solution to a customer's problem. Small teams investigate a number of ideas with a limited amount of time—perhaps one day to construct a working prototype. The ideas that survive undergo another round of rapid prototypes and then, perhaps, another until the team converges on a solution that seems promising enough to take into further development.

Protostorming events begin with focused brainstorming to identify some potential solutions to a specific design challenge. The group includes

FIGURE 4.1
Tom Bachinski in a protostorming session at DJO Global.

product developers, marketing representatives, and a few people who don't typically participate directly in product development. They break into small cross-functional teams to explore the most promising designs. The teams have a set period of time to deliver a working prototype and then report what they've learned back to the entire group. Ideas that survive the first round may go through a second round of refinement. Eventually, the team converges on a single concept that it will investigate.

Although DJO has invested in rapid prototyping tools, the main materials in a protostorming event include cardboard, duct tape, and components from existing products (Figure 4.1). The idea is to build a working prototype as fast and cheaply as possible. Passion and creativity count for more than style, and design specs, if any, come at the end of the process—not the beginning.

LAMDA AND A3 PROBLEM SOLVING IN PRODUCT DEVELOPMENT

A visitor to DJO's R & D labs near San Diego, California, cannot help but notice that the walls are covered with a variety of A3 reports. At some point, the company's engineers even developed a special system to hang these A3s on the walls so that they could be taken down easily to update or bring into a meeting. These A3s support a PDP that is built around learning cycles.

Problem-solving A3s support good systematic problem solving by encouraging collaboration and visualization. The problem solving A3 captures the problem solver's current thinking about the problem and potential solutions. It is meant to be shared as soon as the first section, the problem statement, gets drafted. Sections on the problem solving A3 template guide the problem solver to make observations about the current state, analyze the root causes, develop multiple alternative solutions, and get constant feedback before committing to a recommendation. At the same time, the problem solving template is not a straitjacket; the problem solver can add, subtract, rearrange, and resize elements of the A3 report to fit the needs of a specific problem, as long as he or she can justify the changes with a good A3 that tells the story of the problem solving process and the resolution.

A3 REPORTS: WHAT AND WHY

Many of the companies featured in this book have incorporated A3 reports into their Lean Product Development programs. The first question people usually ask is, "What is an A3?" An A3 is an especially effective communication tool for supporting the systematic problem solving and selectively standardized work that we encourage in a Lean environment. Over time, A3 reports replace PowerPoint® slide sets, lengthy text documents, and e-mail chains as the primary means for communicating knowledge and ideas within a Lean organization.

The A3 refers to the paper size: 11 × 17 inches in the United States and 297 × 420 mm everywhere else. It turns out that this paper size is especially conducive to developing reports that are concise yet rich in content. The next smaller size—A4 or letter size—is simply too small. Any larger paper size is unwieldy. Any report that is double sided, especially two pages front and back, hides some of the information all the time.

THE FIVE TYPES OF A3 REPORTS

The original research into Toyota's processes classified their A3 reports into three types: the Problem Solving A3, the proposal A3, and the Status Reporting A3. I have found that there are five different kinds that Lean organizations primarily use. I've listed them from the most free form to most standardized in format:

- **Knowledge Capture A3s,** sometimes called knowledge briefs or K-Briefs, are reports about some area of knowledge that the author wishes to share. I have seen excellent examples of Knowledge Briefs written about test procedures, market forecasting methods, platform architecture models, and many others. To make a good Knowledge Brief, the author needs the flexibility to use the space on the page in whatever way will best suit the subject matter.
- **Problem solving A3s** document systematic problem solving and support LAMDA/PDCA cycles. Good Problem Solving A3s tell a story about the problem, the analysis, and the recommendations.
- **Proposal A3s** resemble Problem Solving A3s in the sense that they document the solution to a problem, and many proposal A3s began as Problem Solving A3s. But the purpose of a proposal A3 is to get a specific decision to implement a specific recommendation. The focus shifts from analyzing the problem to executing the solution. The Proposal A3 contains information about risks, resources required, and an implementation plan.
- **Documentation Replacement A3s** replace standard reports with a streamlined report that fits on an A3. The purpose of the Documentation Replacement A3 is to communicate precisely what the readers of the report need to know, with nothing extra. Examples of documentation replacement A3s include product and technology road maps, product portfolios, product program charters, technical specifications (usually a series of A3s grouped by topic), market forecasts, business case analyses, team resource allocations, validation plans, localization plans, customer visit reports, etc. Documentation Replacement A3s usually have standard templates.

- **Status Report A3s** reduce project management overhead by streamlining status reports. Unlike the other A3 forms, the Status Report A3 benefits from as much standardization as possible. People who must review multiple status reports from many different people and/or teams benefit from having the same information in exactly the same place.

PROBLEM	TITLE AND AUHOR
CURRENT STATE	DATA AND ANALYSIS
ROOT CAUSE ANALYSIS	RECOMMENDATIONS
EXPERIMENTAL METHODS	NEXT STEPS

Problem-solving A3 report.

As DJO's Lean Product Development practices have matured, they have placed more emphasis on the importance of solving technical challenges systematically and capturing the knowledge created immediately so that others in the company can benefit from it. Unlike most of the documentation in a typical product development process, A3 reports are meant to be shared as works in progress, which ensures that developers get feedback before they have gone too far down a path that won't work. Some of the best A3 reports I've seen over the years have been handwritten with crude sketches. The finished A3 only needs minimal work to be stored as a piece of reusable knowledge for future product development teams.

In addition to the standard problem solving A3 and the SKU A3 mentioned previously, DJO's product development process has a number of A3s that serve as replacements for the complex documentation that other product development organizations require their engineers to write:

- **Technology Road maps** outlines the key areas of development for DJO's core technology areas for the next several years.
- **New Concept Definitions** defines the customer need, market opportunity, and technical challenges for a concept that is under investigation.
- **Project Status Reports** summarizes the key status information about a project.
- **Vender Background and Capabilities Reports** share the outcome of an investigation into a new vendor's ability to meet DJO's needs.
- **Kaizen Event Objectives and Plans** define the goals, purpose, targets, core parameters, and team for a kaizen blitz.
- **Knowledge Capture Reports** captures knowledge in reusable form.

DJO's PDP model incorporates the A3s right into the process (Figure 4.2). These A3s work together to keep documentation and approvals at a minimum, keep the most important information about R & D activities visible to everyone at all times, and facilitate more productive meetings. Problems can lurk undiscovered in project documentation that is overly complicated and lengthy and that contains a lot of boilerplate language. On an A3, problems have no place to hide.

METRICS TO DRIVE A LEAN PRODUCT DEVELOPMENT CULTURE

Early in DJO's Lean product development program, Rich recognized that all of the measures used to characterize product development performance were lagging indicators. It took a long time for a change in the product development process to show up in these metrics. Most companies start Lean Product Development because they want to increase the number of new products released per year, shorten the lead time for a new product, increase the percentage of revenue from new products, and reduce costs in the product and in R & D itself. If a typical product development project takes three years, it will be at least four years and probably five or more years before any incremental improvement efforts change these numbers.

Rich said, "These metrics didn't give me what I needed as a manager to ensure that my teams were doing the right things. I needed some metrics that would give me firm line of sight on the things that would lead to better performance." He developed some new metrics to serve as leading indicators. These metrics captured the activities and behaviors that contribute to a Lean Product Development culture:

- The number of go-and-see events that the engineers organize and attend to visit production facilities, key venders, and customers.
- The number of knowledge capture events.
- The number of concepts considered in early development (more is better to increase knowledge creation).
- The number of core team changes over the life of a program (fewer is better).
- The percentage of time spent on value-added activities versus non-value-added activities.
- The number of R & D process kaizen blitzes.

It may seem silly to track the number of kaizen blitzes when one great blitz can eliminate a lot more waste than a bunch of small ones. This metric can be a problem if a Lean program consists only of kaizen blitzes and employees are not encouraged to use systematic problem solving the rest of the time on the problems that arise every day. People can get the impression that they are only expected to solve problems and eliminate waste within the context of a kaizen blitz, and that they can forget about it the rest of the time. DJO didn't have this problem because the metric was only one of several measures to drive systematic problem solving within R & D.

The guiding principle behind all of these metrics is to make progress visible. The metrics ensure that the product developers have ample opportunities to participate in efforts to improve the product development process, that Rich sees these activities as part of the work of product development, and that the participants get credit for the time they spend on these activities. Dave Packard, founder of Hewlett Packard, often said, "What gets measured gets done."

RESULTS AND NEXT STEPS

For DJO, the ability to see value and waste provided a rich source of ideas for how to increase the amount of time that people spend on value creation.

Before the first book had been written about Lean Product Development, DJO had already begun to develop design blitzes and protostorming and to identify methods to eliminate non-value-added activities from product development. After years of work, the company has cut time to market by 60% from where it began in the late 1990s; it can get more than three times the number of products completed.

In true Lean fashion, DJO does not believe that it has reached a state of perfection. Rich says, "We've come a long way, and we see that we can go even further." The company has emphasized the A3 report as a template for improving communication across the R & D organization. It has experimented with ways to improve project management across sites with visual planning tools that work in a virtual environment. DJO believes that it has just begun to reap the benefits from actively managing the knowledge creation value stream.

Meanwhile, DJO's success has allowed the company to purchase related companies to help it grow even faster. Rich's next major challenge is to transfer all of the knowledge and experience built in San Diego to new development sites in Texas, North Carolina, and Switzerland.

Discussion Questions

- When do your product development teams start building prototypes? What do they learn from the prototype builds?
- What types of documentation are most prevalent in your organization? Where could things be streamlined?
- How do you measure product development performance today?

Next Actions

- ☐ Track your time for a week to see how much of your time is spent creating value. (You don't have to show this to anyone—especially not your manager!)
- ☐ Estimate the cost per hour of meeting time for the meetings you attend regularly. Do they create enough value to justify the expense?
- ☐ Write a Problem Solving A3 about a problem that is within your control to solve. The LPDRC has examples and templates to give you some ideas.

WHAT ABOUT TOYOTA?

I mentioned in Chapter 2 that Toyota was not viewed as an innovative company today. That would have been reason enough to exclude Toyota from this survey, but I chose to exclude Toyota from the Lean Product Development Benchmarking Study for three other reasons:

1. Toyota's product development practices have already been well documented in other books, especially *The Toyota Product Development System* by James Morgan and Jeffrey K. Liker.
2. We already know what Lean Product Development means at Toyota and that it works for them. I wanted to know what was happening inside companies that were using Lean Product Development principles to transform their product development systems.
3. I was most interested to see whether or not Lean Product Development practices could generate sustainable results when they lack the support of a Lean Enterprise infrastructure (or when that infrastructure was not necessarily conducive to Lean Product Development).

5

Scania Technical Centre: A Pioneering Lean Product Development Champion

Scania is known worldwide for its modularized heavy truck and bus line, which allows the company to deliver special-purpose vehicles with high degrees of customization from a limited number of main components. I first learned about Scania's modular designs in 1997 from H. Thomas Johnson, author of *Profit beyond Measure*. Dr. Johnson was a professor in my MBA program. It was the first presentation I saw about Lean Thinking applied to product development, although Dr. Johnson didn't use those words at the time.

Scania has been experimenting with Lean ideas since 1990, and it cooperated with Toyota during the mid-1990s to understand the Toyota Production System that is at the core of Lean manufacturing more deeply. The company has always taken a long-range view: Change mind-sets first, then change habits, then change working methods. Its goal was to develop a culture of continuous improvement from the ground up.

LEAN PRODUCT DEVELOPMENT AT SCANIA

Scania has explored how Lean principles apply in product development almost from the beginning of its first Lean projects. In the early 2000s, some R & D managers met with Allen Ward. At the same time, they began to build a team of Lean Improvement Coaches to work with R & D teams. Four Lean Improvement Coaches helped Scania's development teams to adapt Lean methods for their projects.

ABOUT SCANIA TECHNICAL CENTRE

Scania's objective is to deliver optimized heavy trucks and buses, engines, and services that enable its customers to achieve the best operating economy. Scania operates in about 100 countries and has more than 37,500 employees. Research and development activities are concentrated in Sweden. Production takes place in Europe and South America, with facilities for global interchange of both components and complete vehicles. In 2011, invoiced sales totaled SEK 87.7 billion, and net income amounted to SEK 9.4 billion. Their corporate website is http://www.scania.com.

However, they don't call it Lean inside R & D—not even manufacturing uses the term. This is a common issue in product development organizations. In some organizations, the term "Lean" has been used in ways that make the word toxic in product development. Scania's situation was not so extreme—Lean is just something used outside the company. The leaders care less about the use of specific Lean practices than they do about the foundations of systematic problem solving and continuous improvement.

Peter Palmér is a Lean Improvement Coach for Scania's R & D teams. Peter grew up with Scania's version of Lean in its transmission manufacturing facilities in Södertälje, Sweden, from the late 1980s. He also had the opportunity to apply it in the manufacturing of chassis, busses, and transmissions in Argentina. Peter says, "It's easy to push something onto a team but if they have a different need, why should they accept it? In reality, we are pushing the habits and working methods but we don't want them to feel pushed. We try to help the teams understand that this is what they need."

When you observe Scania's R & D factory's model of mission and strategies, the word "Lean" is notably missing. Yet the details show the influence of Lean Product Development: Standardization, visualization, balancing, cross-functional and parallel work, modularization, and demand-driven output all flow out of the principles and practices of Lean Product Development.

This house provides the framework for Scania's culture of continuous improvement. "Right from me" means that my own work is as error-free as I can make it. I don't pass problems down the line to others. "Standardized working method" describes Scania's goal to have the appropriate degree of standardization for a job.

LEAN IMPROVEMENT COACHES

Peter's first year as a Lean Improvement Coach was challenging. At first, it felt like it wasn't working. People didn't understand it. Some members of his team thought they needed to get rid of the managers to get them out of the way. Peter thought it was a better idea to convince the managers to assign representatives from their teams who were 20% dedicated to Lean Thinking. He actively sought people who were perceived to be future leaders, with a strong emphasis on coaching ability.

Peter sought out highly visible projects that would serve as good examples for other teams. He encouraged high-level sponsors to get involved. These pilot projects helped to show the group that these new working methods led to the results that the product development teams needed, and they helped Peter and his team to gain experience themselves that they could leverage across the entire R & D organization. Peter says, "We always had problems with not enough time—but this is a benefit—they'd do too much!"

The goal of an improvement coach is not simply to do training or coaching on specific tools. Instead, Peter's goal is to give the team members the necessary understanding so that they can do things themselves. "They call us and want something, but we usually end up giving them something else. We talk to the managers and ask, 'What problems do you have?' Then we help them solve the problems but we don't take over." A key success factor is their ability to listen for the real needs and the major opportunities.

PRODUCT DEVELOPMENT TEAM ENGAGEMENT

For Peter, the essence of Lean always starts with a culture of problem solving: "If you have a problem, you need to solve it." R & D teams pull Peter in when they have a problem they need to solve and want some help. They don't call him to get training in problem solving; they just want the problem solved. Through solving the problem, the team gets direct experience with problem solving.

Their trainings follow a simple framework. The managers leading the teams start and end the meetings, while Peter and members of his team do the technical training; the managers sum up and determine the next steps. The training is not standardized. Some teams want a structured workshop, and others do better with an open discussion. Sometimes they use process mapping or other tools. One group might want to set up a visual planning board, and another team may have a process problem to solve. In the end, both groups get everything, but they get the concepts in the order that they need them.

The improvement coaches look underneath the problems that the teams think they have to help them find the problems that they do have. For example, on the surface, it seemed as though a coordinator did not have all the part numbers needed for delivery. After a little bit of analysis, it was found that the real problem was faulty test results caused by testing the wrong parts. A new part number system would not have helped.

It's important to Peter that his team of Improvement Coaches stays flexible and responsive. They let the groups decide what they need to do and allow the teams to explore different ways of getting there. It's more important to be focused on their problem solving process versus the specific methods they use. It's GOOD for the team to invent a new way of doing something. Then they say, "This is ours."

At the same time, the coach's role is to steer the team gently toward the methods that have been proven to work at Scania. This gives the team a sense of safety and makes it more likely that the team will get the results it wants. The ability to steer without stepping on the team's own exploration requires sensitivity, listening skills, and deep knowledge about Lean principles.

As the Improvement Coach, Peter is the one who does a lot of the job but never gets the credit. He says, "This is good! Managers get the credit and then take responsibility to keep it going. Without that, it will die when the coaches leave."

PRODUCT DEVELOPMENT LEADERSHIP AT SCANIA

Peter coaches the R & D managers to take the time to go-and-see within their teams. The managers should use visual management tools to see problems as they arise and see those problems as opportunities to get better. They set the standard for continuous improvement in their own organizations.

Lean is not a spectator sport for managers. While they can delegate specific activities and problems to solve, the managers themselves need to be active participants in their teams' problem solving work. That helps the team members see how important this is. To support this, Scania uses a "train the trainer" approach where managers take on responsibility for providing their own teams with some of the training on problem solving and visual management.

The managers are responsible for the "mood" of their organizations: Are problems seen as something to hide, or do we make problems visible? Do we make decisions based on data or do we let our personal feelings get in the way? Do people leave work every day feeling like they have accomplished something that will move them and their teams closer to their goals? Do people get the satisfaction of constantly getting better?

Finally, product development leaders must understand how customers use their products. At Scania, this means that the managers and product development engineers spend a lot of time behind the wheel of a truck.

VISUAL PLANNING

One of the hallmarks of Scania's company-wide Lean implementation is the widespread use of visual planning boards for projects that are more extensive than one might imagine, given how simple the tool is. Designing a new heavy truck is a complex endeavor, and managing an organization with many heavy truck development programs is the type of thing that seems to call out for an enterprise-class database-driven project management system. Yet, Scania tracks all of this with whiteboards, magnetic dots, and sticky notes.

Top management meetings take place in front of a "pulse" board—a massive whiteboard covered with magnetic dots that show key project status indicators as red/yellow/green. The data to populate these boards come from the project teams, many of which use visual planning boards themselves. The project teams have visual project plans, and each subsystem has a visual subsystem plan. Teams may have their own visual planning boards to show their main activities for the next weeks or months.

Figure 5.1 shows the schematic for a project room. Japanese companies call these *obeyas* for "big rooms." These project rooms have all of the key project information displayed on the four walls of the room. One can get updated on the project's most important activities, issues, and investigations by reading the boards on the walls. At Scania, many teams have actual rooms, or parts of walls, or visual boards, depending on the real need of the project team. Other organizations use arrangements of cubicles, hallways, or even rolling whiteboards for their visual plans.

THE LEAN PRODUCT DEVELOPMENT CHAMPION

If a company is serious about building a Lean Product Development organization, someone needs to be in front, leading the leaders. The Lean Product Development Champion is the person responsible for driving the vision for Lean Product Development through the organization, group, or team. The Champion must be a highly respected person within R & D. This cannot be outsourced to a consultant or an internal Lean organization. The Champion must be a trusted source of knowledge, usually a senior technologist, seasoned program manager, or recognized up-and-coming leader. The ideal Champion connects with people at all levels, mentoring new engineers and giving advice to senior leaders. He or she has the ability to create pull for Lean in the beginning, because people have high regard for the Champion's new ideas and deep understanding of the company's product development system.

The most effective champions I've observed have not taken on the title of Lean Product Development Director; instead, they use Lean Product Development to do the work of R & D, leading pilot projects and solving the system-level problems that make development work flow more smoothly for everyone. Sometimes, Lean Product Development work needs a program manager of its own to coordinate all the activities to build an infrastructure for knowledge capitalization, develop a portfolio management process to address overload, and shepherd changes to the product development process through the organization. Unfortunately, this person's ability to influence will be weakened without a direct connection to product development programs. Lean Product Development Program Managers will be most effective when they have support from a network of Champions who stay actively engaged with product development. The Champions network seizes opportunities to model Lean Thinking and mentor others in using Lean Product Development practices in real time.

Here are the roles that a Lean Product Development Champions usually fill:

- **Visionary:** They develop a vision—a target state—for Lean Product Development in their organizations and then share the vision with others. They help the organization see a future where there is less waste, more time for value creation, and a deeper pool of shared knowledge to drive innovation. They paint a picture of delighted customers and executives who trust product development to build great products.

- **Systematic problem solving process owner:** The specific problem solving method matters much less than the fact that an organization has one—and uses it. Champions are responsible for selecting and adapting a systematic problem solving method that will become the core of the organization's work with Lean. They experiment with new methods to deepen their understanding. They serve as exemplars of systematic problem solving and they coach others about when and how to use the practice.

- **Mentor of mentors:** Everyone needs a mentor. Champions mentor three types of people: senior managers, middle managers, and senior technical leads. Senior managers need to see the value of Lean Product Development, how to support it, and when to use the practices themselves on strategic problems. Middle managers and senior technical leads will mentor others on systematic problem solving and work on teams to solve the organization's systemic problems. Champions help them all develop the capability to support, model, coach, and reinforce Lean problem solving.

- **Lean PD knowledge owner:** Champions build and maintain an external network of trusted advisors and peers who face the same problems. They attend conferences themselves and select teams of people to attend the most important ones. These injections of best practices from outside the company can help to speed up progress.

- **Guide:** Champions often lead training programs. But even in a classroom situation, "teacher" is not adequate to describe the champion's role. Rather than simply share explicit information and lead the team through learning exercises, the champion serves as a guide, a fellow traveler who is a few steps ahead and understands the landscape.

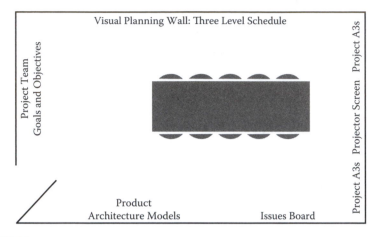

FIGURE 5.1
Schematic of an obeya room.

The visual nature of the planning system reduces the number of reports that have to be written while improving the quality of communication between team members and with partner teams. When a team member, partner, or manager wants an update, he or she can simply visit the room and read the status board. Formal status updates with managers take place in front of the boards. Team meetings and informal working sessions have all the project information they need right in front of them all of the time. They don't have to fire up a laptop to retrieve a project report.

Without the need to spend so much time reporting status, the meetings focus on deviations. Many teams meet in front of their boards on a daily basis to answer four questions: Did I do what I was supposed to do? If not, why? What will I do today? Do I foresee any problems? These daily "PDCA" cycles help the teams rapidly learn what is truly in the way of their work so that they can get more done. They also help the teams learn how to adjust their plans so that they can get more capacity from the same pool of resources. A longer meeting once per week gives the teams a chance to step back from the daily flow of activity to think ahead about the upcoming week.

As teams master visual planning, they learn to break larger activities that are invisible into smaller tasks that make problems surface sooner. They learn by visualizing their process and then figuring out what causes their deviations from the plan. This is only possible if the tasks are small enough. They also learn by reflecting and reviewing in real time and by seeing the results of the improvements every day. Unlike complicated Gantt charts that require project management specialists to create and update, the teams can take ownership for creating their own plans. Because they are the ones who put together the plan, it becomes their plan.

The most important benefit of a visual planning system is that problems have no place to hide. If a person runs into an unexpected problem, a piece of test equipment breaks down, or a key process gets overloaded, the visual planning system brings the problem to everyone's attention immediately. For teams having daily stand-up meetings, issues get raised within one working day, as soon as someone is unable to complete the task he or she had committed for the day before. Every day, team members experience a combination of accountability, assistance with blocking issues, and real-time learning. This helps to pull work through the system faster.

Discussion Questions

- What needs do your company's product design teams have that Lean Product Development could help them with?
- How do you surface problems within product development teams?
- Who develops product development plans in your organization? Who owns them?

Next Actions

- ☐ Go-and-see inside your own development organization. Walk through the cubicle farms, model shops, and test labs. What do you see?
- ☐ Experiment with a visual planning wall for your own weekly activities. Make a simple grid: Rows represent projects or categories and each day of the week has a column. Write the week's activities on sticky notes and place them on the grid. What do you see?
- ☐ Write a problem-solving A3 about how your organization handles project management for product development programs. Where is the value, where is the waste, and how could you improve its effectiveness?

IRWIN SEATING COMPANY'S LEADERSHIP OBEYA

Company: Irwin Seating Company in Grand Rapids, Michigan, makes stadium and auditorium seating for the world's premier entertainment venues.

Problem: Irwin's directors and executives needed to get better visibility into the company's product development projects to make better strategic decisions about how to balance new product development work so that they could provide more useful guidance to the product development teams during status review meetings.

Countermeasure: The engineering group set up an obeya room right off the factory floor, with dedicated space for each project team to show progress. The pictures in the following figure show a schematic of the room and a sample project board. Executives, directors, and the engineering team use the room for decision meetings and weekly status updates. When a team requests capital investments, the decision makers sign the A3 on the wall when they grant approval. Because key project information is visible, everyone knows what the signatures mean.

Results: The room has been in place for more than two years. Bill Peless, the obeya room's owner, said, "It helps make our progress visible, and makes the reasons why we've made decisions more visible. It helps the team see why things happen, and that helps everyone make better decisions."

Next steps: Their understanding about how to benefit from it has continued to evolve. Bill said, "For the first year or so, it was just an update room, but now it's more of a working room. Some project teams meet in here now, and the other functional areas come by to see what's changed on the walls." In their next revision, the group will add a new type of planning board to help them balance capacity across projects and see if they can find windows of opportunity for small projects.

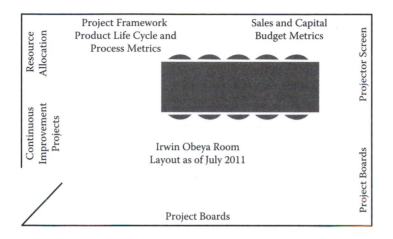

Irwin Seating's leadership obeya.

6

Ford Motor Company: How to Revitalize an American Icon

For over 20 years, the American auto industry has had to manage intense foreign competition in its core markets. During the 1990s, highly profitable truck and SUV sales buffered the Big Three from the effects of foreign competition. By the early 2000s, Toyota and others had begun to infiltrate this market as well, leaving American automakers with little room for error. After world financial markets crashed in 2008, drying up consumer and business credit, the domestic auto industry in the United States was in trouble. The heads of the three major auto companies—GM, Ford, and Chrysler—were criticized for traveling to Washington, DC, in private jets while their companies teetered on the edge of bankruptcy. Ultimately, it took a massive bailout to save GM, and Chrysler was sold to Fiat.

Only Ford was able to move independently through this crisis, largely on the strength of a revitalized product line. As Ford Engineering Manager Randy Frank recalls, "We needed to revitalize our products to revitalize our company, with few resources, to deliver a best-in-the-world product." They needed to make a quantum leap in quality, become cost competitive, and deliver exciting products into the market at speed. This is the type of multidimensional problem that requires a multidimensional view of Lean Product Development.

It also required Ford to begin treating knowledge as something that should be capitalized. Knowledge capitalization is not an accounting maneuver. It is the conscious effort to understand, capture, share, and use the organization's best available knowledge, whether that knowledge resides in past product designs, CAE models, test procedures, or the brains of the company's most experienced engineers. A company that can

ABOUT FORD MOTOR COMPANY

Ford Motor Company, a global automotive industry leader based in Dearborn, Michigan, manufactures or distributes automobiles across six continents with $136 billion of revenue in 2011. Ford has 164,000 employees and about 70 plants worldwide. For more information regarding Ford and its products, please visit www.ford.com.

capitalize on its knowledge eliminates reinvention and unnecessary design loopbacks. Such a company can also find new opportunities to leverage its knowledge for new markets and new types of products.

One of the key participants in the Ford revolution was Jim Morgan, who led a multiyear effort to reinvent automotive body and stamping development at Ford. The Lean community knows Jim Morgan best for his groundbreaking research into the Toyota Product Development System, which was published in 1996 by Productivity Press as *The Toyota Product Development System*. Fortunately for Ford, Jim knows how to translate these ideas into action. Jim, who is the global engineering director for body and stamping engineering says,

> Our goal was not to copy Toyota's product development system. Toyota served as our inspiration but we wanted to maintain and extend our own strengths, and we wanted to better leverage our incredibly talented people and make better use of our technology. Our goal was to develop Ford's product development system while simultaneously delivering world class products our customers really wanted.

LEAN PRODUCT DEVELOPMENT AT FORD

Automotive development is an incredibly complex, highly orchestrated process to deliver thousands of new part designs internally and from dozens of suppliers in an orderly sequence so that they all come together in the first prototype vehicle and, ultimately, on the final assembly line. When the other equipment manufacturers' and suppliers' personnel are added together, thousands of individual engineers contribute to a new car.

FIGURE 6.1
The Lean Product Development system at Ford.

Jim Morgan's approach to Lean Product Development is summarized in a triangle with three sides: skilled people, process, and tools and technology (Figure 6.1). For Ford, a successful Lean product development transformation would address all of these areas simultaneously. Jim considers all three of these elements to be essential to Ford's Lean transformation.

Skilled People

Jim says, "The best people create the best products." Ford has the pull to attract the best college graduates from engineering programs worldwide. But no matter how well a young engineer did in school, he or she is a beginner in the workplace.

Jim and his team thought long and hard about what it takes to develop a new hire into a highly skilled engineer, capable of making complex decisions autonomously. They developed a road map of assignments, support systems, and learning experiences to set their recent college graduates down the path of mastery, eventually becoming technology leaders themselves. The key to this system is the awareness that only technical leaders are qualified and capable of mentoring people who desire to become technical leaders. Managers cannot simply "manage" performance, but rather must have deep technical knowledge. They must be prepared to guide, coach, and mentor. They must have mastered the technology themselves and possess what Jim refers to as "towering technical competence."

In a traditional product development organization, managers lose their technical skills when they become managers. In fact, at many large companies, this loss of technical knowledge is encouraged so that managers can think more "strategically" about the entire business. However, in

Morgan's organization, they recognize that mastery is a "both/and" rather than an "either/or." Managers with technical depth can make better decisions about the entire business. And when it comes to the most important aspect of management—developing the people in the organization—there is no substitute for a manager with a deep understanding of the technology who can help other engineers master the essential elements of their work. This is the type of manager who can make decisions that capitalize upon the best available knowledge within the organization.

Ford developed a system of "technical maturity models" that defined the skills needed for every engineering discipline in every phase of product development, and then it translated that into the specifics that an individual needed to master in order to become a competent engineer. The company designed a rotation program for new hires that ensures that every engineer gets experience in the major areas of his or her discipline and understands what it takes to work within the Ford product development system. Then individuals set development goals with their managers, who work to give the engineers the experiences they need to continue to grow their technical knowledge.

Design reviews also play a key role in developing engineers. In many companies, design reviews are "check the box" exercises that don't contribute much value to the quality of the design. Or they are the opposite: Engineers have to defend their decisions in a confrontational setting that doesn't help the engineers learn why they've made mistakes.

At Ford, design reviews are opportunities for engineers to get good feedback and learn from each other. Since the standard knowledge is embedded right into the system, it's less about identifying mistakes like that. It's more collaborative than confrontational. The reviewers examine innovative approaches from multiple perspectives so that they can be improved. Along the way, the less experienced engineers get insights into the thought process that an experienced engineer uses to evaluate their designs. They learn how to think like experienced engineers. This is the essence of mastery.

Process

I have seen a lot of competent engineers in impossible situations because the product development process was broken. Because every car contains thousands of parts, product development within the auto industry is usually heavily weighted with processes, documentation, and bureaucracy. In 2006, Jim worked with a team to eliminate waste and maximize value in the product development process itself. The team used value stream mapping as a key tool to help its members understand the current state of the product development process and then develop future states and identify the gaps to close. They used PDCA cycles to close the gaps and then standardized the process. The result was a new Global Product Development Process.

Product development processes are heavily knowledge driven. This makes it difficult to map them at a detailed level, and activity-based maps don't capture everything that's important in a knowledge creation process. Ford did not rely solely on value stream maps. The team also viewed product development from the perspective of the system architecture: What core bodies of knowledge did it take to deliver a new vehicle? Some of this knowledge is so foundational that the company embedded it into the process itself. How can it recognize this knowledge when it sees it and embed it right into the tools so that it cannot be missed or forgotten? How does the organization spread new technologies and new insights? How can it ensure that every vehicle embodies the best-in-class knowledge?

Any product development process that does not address knowledge transfer quickly becomes all about documents, drawings, and approvals. These represent the artifacts that contain knowledge—not the knowledge itself. The Global Product Development system (GPDS) team devised a knowledge development process to work alongside the product development process. This knowledge development process consisted of a standard architecture, foundation documents, design rules, parameters, CAD templates, and CAE templates to embed core knowledge directly into the process for building all of the components that go into a car. This system translates all of the performance metrics that define a new vehicle into specific design rules that make it easier to figure out how to deliver on a specific metric. This system pulls together all of the available information about how to make a part that is fail safe, manufacturable, high performance, and low cost with a focus on product excellence and creating true customer value.

Prior to this system, engineers got specs but not much guidance about how to design a part. Even experienced engineers benefit when the standard information is available right in the CAD system. They don't have to rely as much upon their own hard drives, their knowledge of their team members' expertise, and their own memory. Instead, they contribute to

WHAT IS REUSABLE KNOWLEDGE?

Reusable knowledge is explicit knowledge that one person has created and captured in one situation so that another person may apply the knowledge in a similar situation. The knowledge must be explicit—that is, it must be written down—so that the presence of the person who created the knowledge is not required. Tacit knowledge—experience-based knowledge—is usually not directly reusable.

Here are some examples of documents that capture reusable knowledge in product development:

- Technical whitepapers and briefings
- Knowledge Briefs
- Templates
- Checklists
- Platform designs
- Code libraries

We create all of these documents to share the things that we have learned with others so that they don't have to learn things the way we did—the hard way.

THE ELEMENTS OF REUSABLE KNOWLEDGE

Sometimes, it seems like people insist upon ignoring reusable knowledge—so they have to learn everything the hard way. While this may seem like a personnel issue, the root cause is usually that the knowledge is not as reusable as it looks. One of the elements of reusable knowledge is missing, and therefore the individual does not trust the knowledge enough to reuse it.

The elements of reusable knowledge ensure that the person receiving the knowledge has all the pieces to decide whether or not the knowledge applies and how far it can be trusted:

- **Understandable:** clear, comprehensive, and concise enough to be digested easily.
- **Believable:** from a trustworthy source known to be accurate.

- **Actionable:** includes reuse instructions, procedures, or recommendations so that the receiver knows what he or she can do with the knowledge that will be useful.
- **Generalized:** includes enough context about how the knowledge was created that the receiver can determine the limits of applicability.

If any of these elements is missing, the knowledge won't be reused as fully as it could be. If the documentation is too complex or too long, it will take less time to recreate the knowledge than to reuse it. If the source is not trustworthy, the knowledge will be discounted or ignored. If there are no reuse instructions or guidelines, the receiver may not understand how to reuse the knowledge and if the knowledge is too specific or there is no context, the receiver will not have confidence that the knowledge applies to the problem at hand.

THE KNOWLEDGE SUPERMARKET FOR SHARING REUSABLE KNOWLEDGE

Knowledge that is difficult to find won't be reused very often. Unfortunately, most "knowledge management systems" share information—not knowledge—because they don't capture the contextual information that supports believability and accessibility. Knowledge supermarkets store the metadata that lead to believability: author profiles and contact information, links to primary data and sources, tags, or keywords to make search results more relevant.

An effective knowledge supermarket functions as a "pull system" for the organization's reusable knowledge: It is easy to access, searchable, and browsable. It is exceptionally easy to add reusable knowledge to the "shelves"—but each piece of knowledge is tagged with the author's name and references. Authors have access to templates, examples, and mentoring to help them capture all of the elements of reusable knowledge.

In companies today, they often take the form of Microsoft Sharepoint® sites, searchable file servers, or internal Wikis. In general, lightweight, flexible systems based on common platforms work better than proprietary systems, and it's best to separate reusable knowledge from product-specific knowledge so that the users don't have to wade through a lot of irrelevant materials to get to the "gold."

and draw from a knowledge base that they can trust to help them build solutions that are much more robust.

While such a system may seem to drive all of the innovation out of product development, the opposite is true: When engineers are relieved of the need to reinvent any of this knowledge, they are free to focus their creative energy on the parts of the design that require new solutions, such as the need to achieve a step change in performance or to figure out how to drive out more cost without breaking any of the other parameters. They have the ability to capitalize on their organization's knowledge to drive innovation.

Tools and Technology

All of this knowledge has no value if people within the organization don't have access to it. The knowledge architecture and process is supported by a full set of CAD/CAE tools that make this knowledge available right when the engineers need it. The standards make it easier to pull together all of the data needed for good simulations and three-dimensional models, with standard analysis methods to help identify problems before the first physical prototype gets made. Core knowledge is embedded right into the design process, where it is hard to miss (Figure 6.2).

These tools help the group standardize the things that need to be standardized. In a product as complex as an automobile, standard solutions to most problems enable the teams to focus their innovation on the specific areas that make a particular car distinct: fuel economy, value for money, luxury, and/or style. Standard solutions are not nearly as likely to cause problems late in development.

Better integration among tools made it possible for CAE modeling tools to draw from common data, making it possible to do three-dimensional modeling earlier in design. The ability to build a full vehicle body-engineering model using reusable CAD templates helps the engineers understand how their ideas would play out in the context of the larger system, much earlier in the process than they could in the past. This makes likely problems come to the surface much faster, and it gives the engineers the

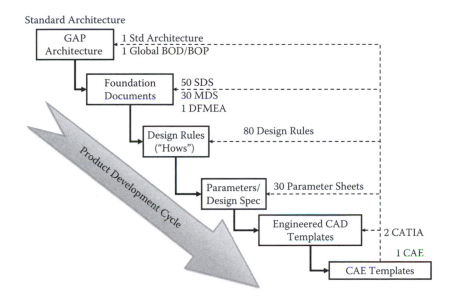

FIGURE 6.2
Standardized knowledge at Ford.

ability to fine-tune part designs to meet rigorous fit-and-finish targets that contribute to the car's overall feeling of quality.

THE CHIEF ENGINEER

Toyota researcher Durward Sobek has often shared a story about the Ford Taurus, circa 1995: A Toyota executive told Durward that "the Taurus is a car with best-in-class components—every part in the car is the best in the world. But it is not a great car. It must have had a weak chief engineer."

Morgan knew from his research into the Toyota Product Development System that the Chief Engineer had a different role in Toyota from that of a typical automotive Chief Engineer. At Toyota, this Chief Engineer performs an integrative function that any complex product needs if all the pieces are going to come together as well as they can. At Ford, there are two types of Chief Engineers: Chief Functional Engineers and Chief Nameplate Engineers. The Chief Nameplate Engineer is the one who takes charge of the overall vehicle. He or she is responsible for ensuring that the different functional areas make decisions that work together. The Chief

Functional Engineer plays this role within a specific function, such as powertrain.

Both of these Chief Engineers pull innovations from the team by setting high standards for delivery and performance. They are technically skilled enough and versed in the organization's knowledge deeply enough that they understand what the current state of Ford's technology makes possible, and where this particular new vehicle will push the envelope. They work in partnership to ensure that the vehicle not only meets the performance standards required to deliver the right new car into the market in the right model year but also that each vehicle program contributes to the overall knowledge base.

EXAMPLE: REDUCING WIND NOISE

As part of the GPDS process, the group created product health charts. These charts predict the areas of greatest technical risk in the project. The product health charts look at core dimensions of quality, including customer-perceived quality. Wind noise is one of those areas that automotive engineers think a lot about so that car owners don't think about it.

Their first product health charts around wind noise showed that they had some significant knowledge gaps in this area. It took them three years, but by systematically closing the knowledge gaps one by one, the team went from one of the worst in the industry to the best on this dimension of quality.

Both existing programs and new programs benefited from this knowledge as it was incorporated into design rules, templates, and simulation models. The new GDPS helped ensure that the entire global organization had access to the insights that reduced wind noise so that none of Ford's customers would ever have to think about it again.

RESULTS AND NEXT STEPS

When I asked Jim to summarize Ford's progress, he said,

In the automotive industry, product is everything. You can't compete without great products and producing a stream of best-in-world products requires a powerful system—anything less than a systems approach will fall short in our environment. There are three key elements to this system: (1) the best people; this means passionate "A players" who have mastered their craft as well as a method to develop them; (2) a Lean process, with a focus on eliminating waste and building in learning and continuous improvement; (3) best-in-world tools and technology designed to improve the process and enhance your people's performance.

In five years, Ford's Lean Product Development work has helped the company surpass its performance benchmarks for quality, lead time, and cost. The company has reduced average overall lead time by 40%, with one all-new car body program delivering nearly 50% reduction. It reduced the time it takes for internal tool and die construction by 50%, on average.

During the same time, Ford reduced internal tool investment costs by 45% and average labor hours per tool by more than 50%. This is a direct result of improvements that have reduced the number of different stamping hits to produce a body part from six to seven hits per part to three to four hits. These changes combine to make Ford Dearborn Tool and Die Plant 400% more productive.

At the same time, the group has improved quality. In a study of vehicle bodies by J. D. Power and Associates, Ford went from the worst of any automaker in 2003 to the best in 2008. It has reduced the number of things that go wrong in the body subsystem by 35% and increased dimensional accuracy by 30%. For the customer, this means less wind noise and better exterior fit and finish.

Finally, Ford has accomplished all of this without alienating engineers, despite severe company-wide downsizing. In fact, morale improved during this transformation. Ford's annual internal survey results for body engineering improved by 30%, as engineers took ownership for the initiative and saw that their innovations were making such a big difference. Jim said, "I'm especially proud of the fact that we were able to get our most talented engineers to take risks and buy in to the new system. As a result, they have contributed innovations that improve cost, quality, and speed."

Discussion Questions

- What professional development opportunities does your company provide to product developers?
- How do the tools and technologies available to you as a product developer support you in delivering products? How do they get in the way?
- What are some of the core bodies of knowledge it takes to deliver your products?

Next Actions

- ☐ Build a visual model of the core knowledge domains that an engineer must master in order to contribute fully to the product development process for your group.
- ☐ Interview your most recently hired engineer to understand how he or she was given the knowledge necessary to be a productive contributor.
- ☐ Volunteer to mentor someone new to your group on who has what information and how to find it.

Section III

Lean Product Development to Make the Right Products

7

Buckeye Technologies: Lean Tools for Strategic Alignment

When I first met Buckeye back in 2008, the main problem they needed to solve was insufficient strategic alignment between the work done in the product and market development organization, and the needs of the project management team. In 2007, this group had experienced a significant product failure when an R & D project that took years of work achieved little to no traction in the marketplace.

Buckeye Technologies is the only global company that makes specialty fibers from wood pulp and cotton. The company uses some of the wood pulp to make nonwoven textiles that go into products like household wipes, high-quality disposable napkins, and tablecloths for restaurants. Its fiber products are a mix of lower tech commodity fibers used in diapers and higher tech specialty fibers that get used in LCD screens, personal hygiene products, and many other applications.

Buckeye makes all of these products in large, complex mills. Its largest facility, in Florida, processes over 450,000 tons of wood pulp fiber every year. These mills have fixed capacity, and the key to profitable growth for Buckeye is to use that capacity to deliver more specialty fiber products that have much better margins. Product development is the key to maximizing profitability in this environment. Yet each new product has to be aligned with the company's overall strategy and market needs.

Buckeye has a long-standing Lean Operations program that uses Lean ideas to improve the company's mill operations continuously. The company had standardized upon an adaptation of the Toyota eight-step problem solving method for systematic problem solving. The executive team had reorganized the company's primary business around the company's three core value streams: wood fiber products, cotton fiber

ABOUT BUCKEYE TECHNOLOGIES

For more than 90 years, Buckeye Technologies Inc. has been a leader in producing value-added cellulose-based specialty products for high-end niche markets worldwide. Its expertise in polymer chemistry and fiber science, combined with advanced manufacturing practices with both airlaid and wet-laid technologies, enables the company to provide the broadest range of products and innovative solutions available today. Their website is http://www.bkitech.com.

products, and nonwoven, with Value Stream Leaders responsible for all the operations in their value streams. Buckeye's Lean Enterprise model calls out Lean Product and Process Development as one of four pillars that support profitable, sustainable growth. Yet product development was not well aligned with the needs of those value streams.

Prior to the first Lean Product Development efforts, responsibility for product development was split among a number of different groups. At the company's headquarters, a Product and Market Development group had primary responsibility for developing new products, while the major manufacturing facilities also had engineers who responded to specific customer requests and sought to optimize the company's production processes. Without a comprehensive view of how product development resources across the company were deployed, it was difficult for the company's executive team to have good control over the projects that people were working on—much less over how it fit with the overall strategic goals of the company.

LEAN PRODUCT DEVELOPMENT AT BUCKEYE

The most wasteful thing a product development team can do is to deliver the wrong product.

Lean Product Development at Buckeye focused first on developing the right products for the value streams. In January of 2009, Buckeye convened product developers from around the company to explore how to get better results from product development. This team had a key breakthrough when they realized that product and process development was a company-wide activity—not something that only Product and Market Development was responsible to do. This enabled Buckeye's management to develop comprehensive road maps for product development that brought all of the group's activities together, whether it was to improve capacity, lower cost, improve quality, respond to a specific customer need, or develop an entirely new product.

The first step to understand the current state was simply to inventory all of the activities that went on at Buckeye that required product or process innovation—no matter where they were done or who did them. A simple map showed that the company had way too much time and money invested in high-risk, potentially high-return projects—and low-risk projects with both high and low returns to support its current business—with not much in between. This map showed that the company would be better off with a balanced portfolio of products that it could sell to markets that were adjacent to the ones it was already in, as well as develop better products.

It also learned that no one at Buckeye had complete visibility into the actual projects that were under way. The projects were split among too many groups, with no overall picture. The company didn't have enough visibility into the financial returns it had received for its product and process development investments.

This team had to figure out how to find, filter, and select the product ideas that would help the company achieve its objectives, and then how to keep track of them in one integrated picture. They decided to go after solutions to two specific problems: how to align product development work to value stream needs and how to pull ideas from the entire organization into the product development process.

SYSTEMATIC PROBLEM SOLVING FOR PRODUCT STRATEGY DEVELOPMENT

Fortunately, this team had a secret strength: All of the leadership team members, including the CEO, President, and the three Value Stream Leaders, were true believers in Lean thinking. They just needed a place to start. Once they had a system in place, systematic problem solving to solve leadership problems was something the leaders could do for themselves. Paul Horne, Senior Vice President of Product and Market Development, took responsibility for developing a new strategic planning process that would build better alignment across the business.

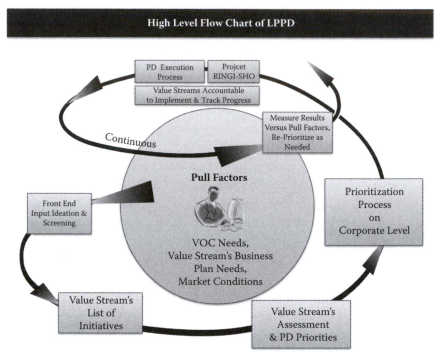

FIGURE 7.1
Buckeye's view of the Lean Product Development system.

Over the next five months, Paul and his team developed a process for strategic planning, ideation, and concept selection that put customer and business needs at the center (Figure 7.1). First, each Value Stream Leader identified the pull factors that were most important to the value stream. Then the group asked Buckeye's people to generate ideas about how to best address the pull factors. The ideas went through several levels of screening to become the value stream's master list of initiatives. The executive team merged and prioritized each of the initiatives or programs onto a single company-wide list of product development activities that clearly aligned with Buckeye's strategy.

THE POWER OF PULL FACTORS

In Lean Product Development, pull factors are the clues that tell a company that it needs a new product. These pull factors can arise from a major customer's need, market conditions, business plans, and voice of the customer. In Buckeye's new strategic planning process, the Value Stream Leaders characterize the pull factors that they see in their markets.

Some examples of pull factors include:

- New market opportunities: ways to leverage a company's technical knowledge into solutions developed for a new market.
- Major customer needs: product improvements targeted for a major customer's future product.
- Cost savings: opportunities to improve the product or the process to lower manufacturing costs for Buckeye and/or its customers.
- Environmental projects: Process improvements to reduce or recycle waste products, consume less energy, or use more environmentally friendly additives in the process.
- Quality improvements: product or process improvements to make the product more consistent and reliable.

Of course, everyone wants to address all of these needs at once. Paul's process forced the Value Stream Leaders to select the critical few, and to prioritize them so that the teams had clear guidance about how to decide between product concepts. With Paul's support, each Value Stream Leader produced an A3 that summarized the most important pull factors for his or her business.

LEAN IDEATION WITH CONVERGENCE

Once the first-pass pull factors had been defined, Jacek Dutkiewicz took responsibility for pulling ideas from the organization about how to best respond to these pull factors. In the spring of 2009, he and his team held a series of ideation sessions with a broad range of people inside Buckeye and at all of Buckeye's major sites. This process generated hundreds of ideas.

Teams of subject matter experts screened these ideas to identify which ones showed the most promise. The ones that passed fell into three categories: "go–do"—an idea that is so easy and so valuable that it needs no further analysis. Cost savings ideas often fall into this category. "Research now" ideas warrant further investigation. "Pending" ideas are held in

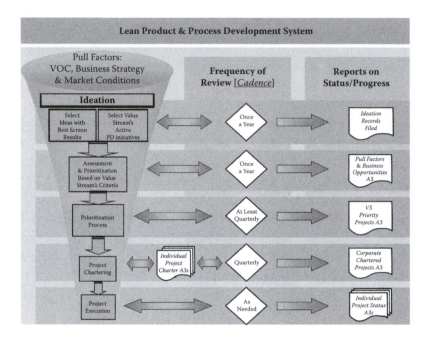

FIGURE 7.2
Buckeye's A3-driven strategy development process.

reserve in case the ones under research don't pan out. Then it was time for the business teams to figure out where to focus first.

The group then developed a series of A3s to guide the business through the process of converging on a plan (Figure 7.2).

- **Pull Factors and Business Opportunities:** Each value stream's pull factors get consolidated onto an A3.
- **Value Stream Priority Projects:** The projects for a value stream, shown in priority order, go on an A3 that is tied to the pull factors. This A3 shows how each proposed project would address the value stream's pull factors, along with how much technical and market risk they have, expected costs, and financial projections.
- **Chartered Projects:** Once projects have passed out of the concept phase into active development, they go onto a master chartered projects A3 that covers the entire company. This A3 summarizes project status information so that the value stream leaders can get one integrated picture of the product development work to support the value streams.
- **Project A3:** Each project has an A3 to report current status.

WHAT IS CONVERGENT DECISION MAKING?

Convergent decision making is a process for making decisions that begins with a set of options and converges to a single decision in a series of convergence steps.

As the figure shows, the options get refined a little more, with less uncertainty at each step. By the end of the process, the final decision has much less risk, and there are several strong backup candidates if the final decision does not work as anticipated. The refinements depend upon the decision to be made: Perhaps a financial model calculates ROI, or a market survey deepens customer knowledge. Each option then must pass through a filter that eliminates the weakest options. For example, a filter might screen out projects with ROI less than 20%.

This is not parallel-path decision making. At each step, the set gets smaller as weak options go away and remaining ones evolve until the strongest one emerges at the end. Only the final candidates justify more than a small investment.

KEYS TO SUCCESSFUL CONVERGENT DECISION MAKING

- Good ideation process to generate options: brainstorming for small decisions, and large-scale ideation for big ones.
- Understanding of the major criteria that any successful options will need to meet, the major risks that need to be understood, how their performance will be measured against the criteria and the risks, and how to test the options.
- Plan to address the easy-to-test criteria first and to refine the options at each convergence step, with explicit filters and time limits. What is the "one more thing" that the team can do to refine the options further at minimal cost and effort?
- Commitment to eliminate only the weak options rather than choose the strong ones. Often, the decision that emerges at the end is an option that was only mediocre at the beginning, but blossomed as it evolved through the convergence steps into the clear winner.

- Commitment to capture all the knowledge created in the process from the options that succeeded and the ones that did not.
- Willingness to truly eliminate options based upon the filters, even the "pet projects" of influential people in the organization.
- Understanding of the timing of the decision and how that relates to other key decisions that the team must make.
- Ideation and refinement processes that do not pit teams or individuals against each other. Competition does not help: Each member of the decision-making team must make data-driven decisions. This is harder to do if members are "attached" to the ideas that they generated and refined.

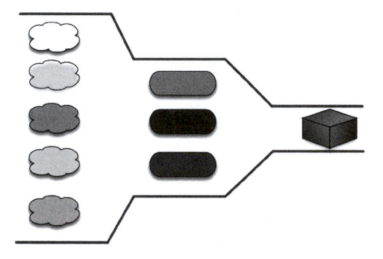

Convergent decision making.

The executive team reviews each of these A3s on a set cadence: Pull Factors once per year and chartered projects quarterly. Project Status A3s are kept up to date so that they can be reviewed as needed. In the three years since this process was put into place, these A3 formats have evolved, but the overall process and structure have proven to be robust. The executives have used similar principles to make the corporate strategic plans more visual, improving alignment between product development plans, capital budgeting, and strategic planning. At the same time, they have been able to reduce the amount of time they spend on strategic planning since the results of the teams are clearer.

RESULTS AND NEXT STEPS

Paul recalls, "When we started, our strategic plans were cluttered and hard to interpret, and our Board of Directors meetings were mostly show-and-tell. Today, we have much more process discipline around strategic planning all the way to the top." Paul showed me some A3 reports that the Board of Directors used in their April 2011 meeting to have better discussions around the company's strategic direction. These reports facilitated a rich conversation with the Board about the most important pull factors, the risks and opportunities, and the countermeasures that the business would use to address them. The reports showed that the group was thinking systematically about the direction of the company, which is the most important problem that they have to solve.

The entire executive team feels more ownership for the success of product and process development projects, whether they take place in the corporate labs or in the mills themselves. The plant members who operate key equipment now see themselves as part of the team. One effect of this process has been to push more of the product development out to the factories and away from corporate headquarters. Since the mills are the places where these new products would need to be produced and since the engineers there have the deepest understanding of each mill's processes, they are the ones in the best position to make simple product modifications to meet customer needs and to experiment with new ways of making product.

President Kris Matula says,

> In the past, we had tacit agreements among the value streams, but not that close alignment that leads to accountability. Today, we have much more internal alignment and the recognition about what it takes to support the entire value stream. We have a fairly short list of good projects—our odds of success are much higher.

Discussion Questions

- How does your company align its strategic objectives with product development projects?
- What are the market pull factors that are most important to your company's business?

- How often does your group's product development portfolio get reviewed? Is that often enough—or perhaps too often?

Next Actions

☐ Interview one of your business partners, such as a person who represents sales and marketing on product development teams. Ask him or her which pull factors are most important.

☐ Map out your company's current portfolio on a 2 × 2 matrix with risk on one axis and expected return on the other. How much risk is your business carrying?

☐ Examine your current product development project from the perspective of market pull: Why does your company need to make this product? Where is the pull for it? If your project does not appear to have a strong pull from the market, perhaps it's worth the time to define the product's pull factors.

THE PRODUCT PORTFOLIO MANAGEMENT
PROCESS AT WATLOW

Company: Watlow provides thermal solutions, like heaters, sensors, controls, systems, and software, primarily for industries where it's important to manage the thermal control loop. The family-owned company was founded in 1922 in St. Louis, Missouri.

Problem: Watlow set the goal to achieve growth at a rate that was much faster than the company has historically been able to grow. The company planned to grow by initially focusing more deeply on three key markets: semiconductor processing equipment, diesel emissions reduction, and energy processes. To achieve these targets, Watlow needed to make the most of its development capacity.

Countermeasure: Watlow developed a portfolio management process to balance capacity with opportunity for the creation of new value across the three markets. That required the company's leaders to change their perspective on risk. They embraced the idea that instead of trying to pick the best opportunities, they would need to explore as many opportunities as possible without spending too much time on any of them in order to learn where breakthrough was feasible.

To assist them with this, the Portfolio Management Team built a model that calculates the value of an opportunity by balancing levels of risk. The concepts that did not prove themselves get dropped, and the ones that remain must continue to justify their resources with promising investigations.

Meanwhile, the developers focus their investigations on activities to help the company understand and increase a concept's probability of success. The product developers are aligned around the need to increase the overall value of the company's product portfolio rather than the success or failure of any given concept.

Results: The product portfolio process has been in place for two years in one of the business units. By Q1 of 2012, this unit had a 62% increase in sales and 75% increase in the economic value of the active development projects. They have supported their active projects with a 91% increase in the economic value of the development opportunities that are undergoing early investigation and appear to be worthy of pursuit.

Next steps: Based upon the results of the first business unit, the executive team established a goal of implementing this process in all of Watlow's business units in 2012. As a result, the product portfolio team is learning how to balance standardization and consistency with the flexibility to adapt this process for new situations. They are also continuing to deepen their understanding of how many concepts need to be in early investigation so that they can maximize the economic value of the projects in active development.

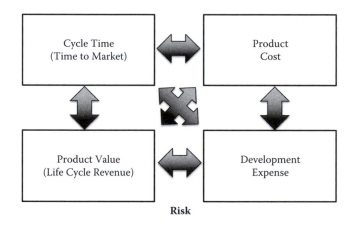

Risk factors for evaluating concepts.

8

Steelcase: Go-and-See New Customers to Open New Markets

Is Lean Product Development the only path to the mastery of innovation?

I said in Chapter 1 that Lean Product Development encompassed a broad range of practices and philosophies, all geared to maximize value and minimize waste. Toyota's production system is justifiably the model for Lean manufacturing. In product development, Toyota also had some great ideas, especially the way that systematic problem solving expressed itself in Toyota's development centers. However, product developers need to look beyond Toyota to other companies that have developed their own ways to maximize value and minimize waste in product development.

Steelcase has just begun to adopt Lean Product Development practices in its product teams, but in one important area, they have already mastered innovation.

Steelcase has independently developed some breakthrough methods that describe how to go-and-see customers in the environments where Steelcase's furniture will be placed, how to distill their observations into a deep understanding of customer value, and how to work effectively as a team, with marketing, design, engineering, operations, finance, and quality all focused on developing the best solutions for maximum customer value. Steelcase developed these abilities in part through its ability to leverage its long-term partnership with IDEO, a design firm based in California that has won more *Business Week*/IDSA Industrial Design Excellence Awards than any other firm. Until 2007, Steelcase was a majority owner, and the company remains a key IDEO client.

Twenty-five years of cross-fertilization between IDEO's and Steelcase's industrial designers and engineers has enriched the Steelcase product line with innovative furniture solutions to foster collaboration among teams,

ABOUT STEELCASE

Steelcase is the global leader in furnishing the work experience in office environments, with $2.4 billion of revenue in 2011. The company provides products and services founded in a research methodology that generates insights about how people work and how spaces can help create great experiences. Its website is http://steelcase.com.

enable flexible workspaces, and build environments that support a workforce that is global, mobile, and team oriented. In 2008 Steelcase built an Education Solutions group to move its innovation process into the education market. As a starting point, the group's General Manager, Sean Corcorran, saw an opportunity to leverage Steelcase's innovation process to reinvent the classroom environment.

LEAN PRODUCT DEVELOPMENT AT STEELCASE

Like many of the companies in this book, Steelcase came to Lean Product Development through Lean Manufacturing. Steelcase first experimented with Lean Manufacturing in 1996. By 2003, Steelcase had achieved enough momentum to launch a corporate-wide Lean Enterprise program. In 2005, Steelcase began moving Lean Thinking into its administrative processes, including IT. In 2010, Tim Schipper and Mark Swets documented their methods for Lean IT development in the book *Innovative Lean Development; How to Create, Implement and Maintain a Learning Culture Using Fast Learning Cycles.* When I visited the company in 2011, they had successfully piloted some of these methods in product development.

Right away, I saw that they already had a deep understanding of customer value and paid more attention to the importance of customer value than anyone else I had visited. They were especially proud of their accomplishments with the "Node chair," which had already become an award-winning best seller in classrooms, a market that was relatively new to Steelcase. They credited that success to the Steelcase/IDEO approach to customer research, which builds a deep understanding of customer needs and provides for frequent feedback between product developers and potential customers.

Some companies struggle with Lean Product Development because they lack a clear understanding of customer value. It's difficult to recognize waste if you don't know what value looks like. Other companies have a deep understanding of customer value—for their current customers. Steelcase has the ability to build deep understanding about new customers and new markets: The company has mastered customer intimacy intelligence. This gives a company the ability to leverage technical knowledge into new growth opportunities.

CUSTOMER INTIMACY INTELLIGENCE IN ACTION

In 2008, as part of a broader focus on education spaces, Steelcase identified an opportunity to reinvent the classroom, just as the company had worked to reinvent the office space. But Steelcase's product designers didn't know much about the classroom—all they had at the beginning was a set of hypotheses. The education market seemed to represent a great opportunity to leverage the process that Steelcase used to innovate in offices into a new arena. Steelcase had always been a strong player in university administration offices, but not in classrooms or libraries. Tim Elms, Product Manager for the Node chair, recalled, "We had tons of information on the office but this was an exploratory focus; we needed to get out to meet our users on campus."

Steelcase decided that its ability to learn about customer needs gave it an opportunity to expand. The company consciously chose not to buy into the market with acquisitions, imports, or licensed products. Instead, it decided to change the game and start from scratch. The group decided to focus first on a new type of chair that would be mobile, so that students could move them around to work in teams or to move from one station to another in a classroom.

The Node team began with a detailed survey to validate some preliminary ideas they had developed for users in a university setting. The key things that came up were

- Swivel seat at a fixed height
- Work surface that was adjustable by the user
- Tripod base for storage

With IDEO's help, the Node team began laying plans to build a chair to pull new buyers in. They felt that this product could demonstrate that traditional desks, tables, and chairs were not the best solutions for the students or the school. They also felt that they could capitalize upon the trend toward more active, team-based learning—not just lecture. More and more classrooms needed to accommodate multiple modes of learning. The Node team felt that they could develop a product that could speak to that, but, first, they would need literally to go back to school.

GO-AND-SEE

All their thoughts about the education market were simply hypotheses until Steelcase undertook a project to go-and-see. A research team set off to do some fundamental research about teaching and learning. Team members sat in classrooms at local high schools and at the University of Michigan for hours and hours. They interviewed deans, superintendents, architects, purchasing agents, registrars, facilities managers, teachers, and students. One notable quote from a dean inspired the team: "I have a vision that all classrooms will support active learning"—meaning more flexible and engaging. A facilities manager said, "I have to get 70 students in there, and then I have to clean the floors. It's not about maximizing occupancy. It's about maximizing utilization." Here are some of the customer values they identified:

- **End users (both students and teachers):** more comfortable, adjustable to fit students better, with a place to store stuff
- **Lecturer/teacher:** able to rearrange at will, not tripping over student stuff left on the floor
- **Purchaser:** warranty, contracts
- **Architects:** help them look like the experts by helping them to leverage Steelcase's research and expertise
- **Designers:** contemporary, sustainable, colorful
- **Facilities managers:** Easy to clean; easy for the classroom to be cleaned

One of the surprising things the team discovered was that rolling chairs made it much easier to clean the floors than stackable chairs. Stacked chairs have to be stacked, then moved, then moved again, then unstacked. The stacks are heavy, cumbersome, and even hazardous. Chairs with casters could just be rolled, three or four at a time, out into the hallway. This took up hallway space temporarily, but no one cared about that.

VALUE AND PRICE VALIDATION

At the time that Steelcase was exploring this market, there were 40 competitors. Steelcase used the data to develop a pricing schema for its products. It asked people about the features designed into the chair: Were they valuable? Were they worth paying for? At the end, the company calculated that it could charge a small premium over the midrange of the market for this chair based on the new functionality and innovation that Node delivered.

After the preliminary design and pricing process, the team launched beta sites to test out the theories. One tool they used was time-lapse photography. They took pictures of classrooms throughout the day prior to the Node chairs being installed, to see how the instructors, students, and janitors interacted with the existing chairs. Then they took another set with Node chairs in the classroom. That helped them test the realities of their designs. The group validated their findings with users at every step. "By the end, we came to believe that we had a market looking for a product versus a product looking for a market," Tim Elms said.

VALUE-DRIVEN DESIGN

The overall product design itself underwent 50 iterations. Students were invited to come in and test some of these interim designs—to put their backpacks underneath the chairs to check out the storage space, to sit and roll around in the chairs. Tim recalls, "We tried a lot of different features before settling on the final design." It was important to cull out the ideas that truly contributed to customer value versus just being good ideas. Along the way, IDEO supported the team with a series of refined concepts and prototypes:

CUSTOMER INTIMACY INTELLIGENCE: THE ABILITY TO CREATE CUSTOMER INTIMACY

Customer intimacy intelligence is the ability to learn about customers. To get it, product developers master the core skills that are required to make the most of a customer interaction: identify specific customers, make observations, conduct interviews, set up early-look feedback sessions, and coordinate go-and-see visits. Once product developers have mastered these skills with their current customers and products, it becomes much easier for them to learn about new markets and to engage with customers about future needs as well as current needs. When this is a core competency, the organization gains the ability to investigate a new market in the way that it can investigate a new technology. Since teams have the ability to see the drivers of customer value, new products for new markets have less market risk, and the company strengthens its ability to grow.

TO BUILD TRUE CUSTOMER INTIMACY, GO-AND-SEE

Lean problem solving drives us to go to the source. The source of customer intimacy is with our customers. To build deep customer knowledge, we need to go-and-see for ourselves. If it were possible to build customer intimacy through databases of sales history, it would not be so difficult to make decisions that impact customer value.

As with any other kind of knowledge, the explicit part is the tip of the iceberg. If we truly want to understand customer needs, especially all the needs they cannot easily express, we need to be able to build a base of experiences that give us the ability to put ourselves in their shoes. It's the tacit knowledge that we build through direct customer interactions that helps us make the decisions that maximize value for everyone. That is where we get the products that customers truly enjoy.

Not every product developer needs this direct experience. The people who are responsible for driving the vision for a product definitely need it, as does anyone in a position to decide among trade-offs that include drivers of customer value. For all but the simplest products, technical staff need these experiences just as much—if not more—than the people in Marketing, Design, or Human Factors Engineering. Without that direct, personal experience it is hard to understand why these customer representatives make the requests that they do. Technical staff make decisions every day that directly impact customer value. They make better and faster decisions if they have customer knowledge of their own.

At the end of the day, we build customer intimacy customer-by-customer. Surveys, market tests, and sales data can tell us all the easy stuff, but they can tell our competitors the same things. If we can develop the capacity to build personal relationships with sets of current customers, we build a base of customer knowledge that is much less easily copied to maximize the value of our current product lines. If we can build relationships with potential customers, we give ourselves the ability to understand them well enough to deliver the value they need to become part of our ecosystem.

- Easy assembly. The chair is shipped in three parts that assemble in less than 30 seconds without tools, making it easy to get the chairs into a classroom.
- Swivel seats and casters make it easy for students to transition quickly from watching an instructor to engaging a team for group work.
- Personal work surfaces accommodate students in a wide range of sizes, both left- and right-handed, with space for laptops or notebooks. When students move into groups, the workspaces create a "conference table" setting for collaboration.
- Flexible, comfortable seats help students stay comfortable even without upholstery.
- Integrated storage underneath the chairs helps keep stuff off the floor, eliminating trip hazards when students move around the room. And since their stuff is "on-board," there's no downtime from picking up their stuff to move.

Once the design team settled on a single concept (Figure 8.1), the engineering team set out to learn how to make thousands of chairs at a cost that a public high school could afford to pay. All of this research gave the engineers a deep understanding of customer value to help them make trade-off decisions as they built and tested the final

FIGURE 8.1
The Node chair.

design. Along the way, the group had some specific design challenges
to overcome:

- **Ergonomics:** The observers noticed that students presented a wide
  range of body types in high school and college. Pressure maps are
  one way that Steelcase assesses how comfortable a chair is likely to
  be. Pressure mapping showed that the original design was too small.
  The chairs needed to be 1.5 inches (3.25 cm) wider to be comfortable
  enough for a wide range of students.
- **Durability:** Anything that goes into a classroom gets subjected to a
  lot of wear-and-tear. In beta testing, the team learned that one of the
  fasteners on the chair kept coming undone under the stresses of the
  classroom environment. This required the engineers to redesign this
  part for the rigors of the education market.
- **Integrated storage:** A key breakthrough came when the group final-
  ized the design for the base of the chair (Figure 8.2). Rather than
  attaching a storage basket to the legs, the legs and storage basket
  became one integrated unit. This approach made the business case
  work by lowering cost and increasing durability simultaneously.

The final result was a simple design that distilled the essence of customer value into an affordable product that would also deliver maximum

FIGURE 8.2
The Node chair base.

business value. Sean said, "The chair succeeded because we had a good understanding of the customer value that the whole team shared."

RESULTS

The product was launched in June of 2010 at NeoCon, where it won an innovation award. By launch, Steelcase had already received nearly 5,000 preorders. After product release, the Node chair took on a life of its own. Students began asking for the Node chair. After trying the Node chairs, one student said, "The only reason I've been able to deal with the other chairs is because I am a kid."

Steelcase is leveraging everything it learned from the Node chair into new products to support an active learning environment. It wants to move beyond chairs to reexamine all of the elements of the classroom. Sean said, "I am pleased to hear the many testimonials, from teachers, facilities managers, and especially students, about how Node has dramatically improved their classroom experience."

Discussion Questions

- What do you do to help you understand customer value?
- Who are the customers in your customer chain? What values does each customer group need? Where are the needs complementary and where do they conflict?
- When is customer feedback integrated into your product development process?

Next Actions

- ☐ Go-and-see a customer. Spend a day observing people use your product as they use it.
- ☐ Talk to a team that's in early development about how to incorporate more go-and-see visits into the investigation plan for their concept.
- ☐ Map out your customer's value stream, using some simple boxes and arrows. Where is the waste? What is the true value?

CROSS-PROJECT KNOWLEDGE SHARING AT RUAG SPACE

Company: RUAG Space is the biggest independent supplier of space equipment in Europe, with facilities in Switzerland, Austria, and Sweden.

Problem: RUAG Space's R & D teams in Gothenburg build space equipment for specific customers on a project basis. The engineering teams tend to think about their work in terms of these projects, which limits their thinking around the ability to reuse knowledge across projects. The engineers focus on delivering exactly what the specific customer wants, without thinking about how the knowledge they create could be reused, and sometimes suboptimizing the system's ability to reuse knowledge. As a result, these projects take more time than they would if the engineers were able to eliminate this waste of reinvention.

Countermeasure: RUAG Space in Gothenburg held a series of workshops to talk about the concept of "product" by using examples outside RUAG. The importance of including all parts of the organization to help the engineers think beyond their own boxes was discussed. The workshop leaders used a visual model to help product developers think about the need to reuse knowledge across products. This picture shows the flow of knowledge from one product to another as the technology evolves. At the end of the workshop, product developers filled out a questionnaire to ask them about the current state of product development and their desired future state. The leaders organized the answers within the four capabilities, and then they analyzed the gaps between current state and future state. They established action plans to close the gaps.

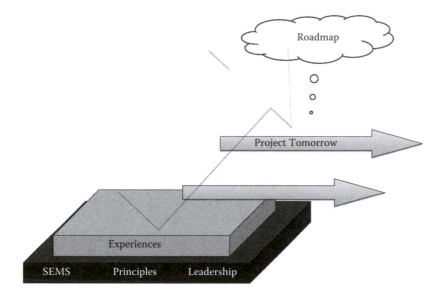

Cross-project knowledge sharing at RUAG. SEMS is RUAG's management system.

Results: Three of the actions have already helped RUAG share knowledge across projects more effectively. The group began conducting technical knowledge sharing seminars to ensure that the product developers would have opportunities to talk about the knowledge they had created with members of other project teams and provide a forum for resolving challenging technical problems.

The group changed the process for analyzing and managing risk and introduced continuous "lessons learned" sessions as a part of every week's project meetings. They support the lessons learned process with a template to guide the reflection and an improvements board to keep track of the improvement ideas.

The group also set up an internal Wiki to capture knowledge. Wikis are internal "Wikipedias"—Intranet systems that use Wikipedia's open-source software to build internal knowledge supermarkets. Per Malmborg, Lean Manager for RUAG Space in Gothenburg says, "The Wiki has grown very strong within some parts of our organization. We see teams using it to share knowledge. For the group, it has become a good tool to share ideas."

Next steps: The company intends to finalize what it has started and continue to work the items that show up on its improvements board. It also needs to figure out how to develop a similar experience for its engineers.

9

Philips: Comprehensive Lean Scheduling

In 2006, Royal Philips Electronics Consumer Lifestyle's Innovation—Personal Care, Drachten, the home of Philips Shavers, found that their customer call rate was unacceptably high. Like many product development teams, they also found that they spent more than expected on development and took longer than planned. In a highly competitive consumer market, those results were a real problem. Suzanne van Egmond says, "Our call rates were too high; we had millions of shavers on the market—a few percent is already a lot of products being returned. Even a small change would make a big difference but we wanted a big change."

They tackled the call rate problem first with Design for Six Sigma tools to improve product quality, better consumer testing, and a deeper understanding of how customers interacted with their products. That helped bring the call rates down, but did nothing for the group's development efficiency and effectiveness. As is typical for consumer electronics, Philips never missed the ultimate launch date but its development costs would, in case of issues, go out of control in the late stages of development, and quality problems would sometimes go unresolved until after launch.

Philips already had a strong Lean program in its manufacturing organization, and in 2007, the company had begun to look at Lean Product Development within the management team. It experimented with a few Lean Product Development ideas, such as the creation of design rules. The group made steady progress, but lacked focus because it was done alongside the operational responsibilities of the management team members.

In September of 2009, the group decided to assign a project manager, Suzanne van Egmond, to speed up the implementation of Lean Product Development. In April of 2010, she was put in charge of Business

ABOUT ROYAL PHILIPS ELECTRONICS

Royal Philips Electronics of the Netherlands is a diversified health and well-being company, focused on improving people's lives through timely innovations. Philips employs approximately 128,000 employees in more than 60 countries worldwide. Innovation Personal Care, Drachten, is responsible for Philips's male grooming and Vitalight products. Learn more at http://www.philips.com.

Improvement for Innovation Personal Care. Her mission was to bring Lean Thinking into product development. Suzanne said, "My managers expected me to really connect to the issues within the organization: to make problems visible and address them in a focused manner building upon the knowledge and experience with Lean Product Development within the company and outside."

LEAN PRODUCT DEVELOPMENT AT PHILIPS CONSUMER LIFESTYLE

Figure 9.1 shows the visual model that the management team created to capture their understanding of Lean Development principles. This

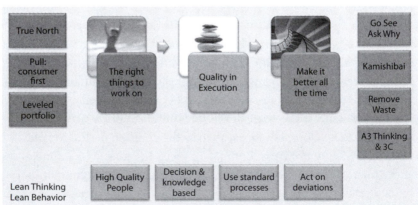

FIGURE 9.1
Philips's Lean Product Development model.

model gave the team a place to start answering the question, "What is Lean Product Development?" Concepts like "the right things to work on" and "quality in execution" are things that everyone can agree with, but it's much harder to decide which things are the right things or how to measure quality in a product development environment. The group was going to have to get much more specific.

Suzanne and her team distributed a set of books to their developers to build a common understanding of Lean Product Development, and managers provided top-down support for product development teams to pilot ideas. The group used value stream mapping, which helped them identify some quick improvements and characterize the root causes they saw in late development. At the same time, the ideas that came out of these sessions did not always get implemented when people went back to their daily work. The connection between Lean and product development was not clear enough.

There is nothing more specific than the development plans for a specific project team. As Suzanne and her team investigated the problems in product development, they began to recognize that the project plans themselves could serve as a leverage point to reinforce Lean ideas, eliminate common forms of waste, and provide a platform for experimentation.

LEAN SCHEDULING

Their investigation discovered that project teams used a lot of different ways to plan their projects. Some teams used detailed schedules, while other groups only planned the major milestones. Planning in many cases led to problems in project execution. The plans quickly got out of date and became unreliable as sources of information about a team's progress. Since project managers developed the plans, the teams did not have much visibility into how the plans were developed and did not take ownership for living up to the plan. It was no surprise that the plans that did exist often fell apart in mid-development.

One key finding was that product developers often had to fight fires because their stakeholders reconsidered key decisions. In fact, a fire in one place could trigger a fire someplace else, simply because the team lost focus on the entire project and accidentally started a new fire while they put out the original fire. Suzanne says,

We came to the conclusion that plans should make sure that decisions within the project are made at the right level of quality, at the right time to prevent wrong decisions. This way, the product developers have a steady flow of work rather than running from one problem to the other.

After a number of pilot projects, Suzanne and her team developed a system of Lean Scheduling that every product development team in her group uses to manage a product development program. The first barrier to overcome was simply the need for a plan in the first place. Product developers often complain that their work is so variable and fuzzy, especially in early development, that plans are useless. They don't know how long it will take them to come up with solutions to the technical hurdles they have to overcome, and they don't know what changes Marketing is going to ask for at the last minute.

Suzanne resolved this problem by having four levels of planning with different levels of detail (Figure 9.2) that are clearly connected:

Level 0 is the Milestone Schedule. It outlines all of the major milestones and checkpoints that the project team must hit if they are going to release on time, and aligns with the company's stage gate process. Depending upon the scale of the project, Level 0 may have months or quarters as its timescale, and it is the tier that varies the least from project to project. Level 0 is a decision-driven plan with the explicit goal of keeping unnecessary documentation to a minimum. It may be stored in a project management tool to produce a nicely formatted printed report and updated infrequently.

Level 1 is an overview of the Key Decisions for the project. Unlike Level 0, Level 1 is built specifically for each project. Every Level 1 looks different. The key decisions are defined and put in a sequence and relation to each other to build the development logic. The team will identify the knowledge required to make each of the decisions, leading to work packages (sets of activity to acquire the knowledge) at Level 2.

Level 2 shows the Major Activities and Deliverables over the next two to three months that the team needs to complete in order to hit the next major milestone or checkpoint, shown on a gridded time line with the weeks running across the top and subteams in horizontal bands. An activity or deliverable is placed in the week when it needs to finish, or a team may have bars that run across weeks showing the entire duration of an activity. This plan may be either computerized or constructed using magnets, sticky notes, and whiteboards. It gets

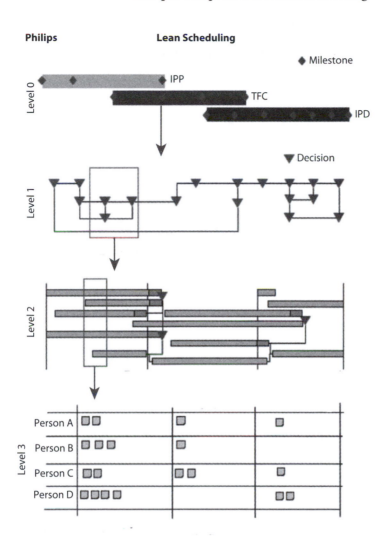

FIGURE 9.2
Levels of Lean Schedules.

updated once per month, when the team adjusts the plans already made for the first two months and then adds the third month.

Level 3 is the Detailed Plan, and it only goes two to three weeks out. This plan shows the immediate action items that the team is working on right now, in order to finish the major activities and deliverables of Level 2 on time. It may be in the form of a gridded time line with days across the top and sticky notes to represent tasks, or it may be kept as a simple list with the action item, owner(s), and due date. This list gets updated frequently—as often as every day and at least once a week.

VISUAL PROJECT PLANS

Good visual project plans have these common elements:

- Visual project plans have a home, and all stakeholders know where it is. The home is big enough to keep the most essential team information visible without having to open anything or look behind anything. The home can take many forms. It could be a physical home such as a dedicated conference room or a virtual home such as a team website.
- Visual project plans include only the information essential to running the project. If a tool doesn't apply, it's not included. This is in direct conflict to most standard product development processes that consist of lists of deliverables to be produced for each phase, sometimes ordered into a prepopulated Gantt chart. It is amazing how much time a project manager can spend updating and maintaining these deliverables.
- The information flow of the visual plan is evident in the layout and structure of the plan. It is clear how the project goals will accomplish the team's mission, and how milestones will drive accomplishment of the goals. Tasks at one level relate to the tasks at levels above and below. In a well-designed visible plan, a person new to the project can start at one corner of the plan and follow the flow of information to the end. By the time someone has read the entire plan, he or she also has a good grasp of the project.
- Visual project plans answer the "why" question as deeply as they answer "what" and "how" questions. This is important for keeping the team in alignment, especially as the project enters into its busiest phases when it is easy to forget the reasons that the project was funded. The project team's goals and objectives are kept front and center so that the team has the constant reminder that this project is linked to real business results. This helps them make the right decisions.

- Visual project plans make things visible. Wherever possible, diagrams and graphs replace descriptive text and numbers. Bullet points replace paragraphs. Simple models replace complex charts. Anything that represents information overload tends to get weeded out of a visual project plan.

One of the major problems with project planning in product development is that the volume of changes is overwhelming. If one attempts to track a product development program of any complexity using Gantt charts, a weekly status update can require hours of work by the project manager to bring the Gantt chart in alignment with current reality. Since Gantt charting software automatically adjusts everything as the schedule changes, milestones get moved that shouldn't be moved, sometimes without the project manager or the team noticing that dates have changed. This encourages product development program managers to avoid detailed planning, which makes it easy for schedule risks to go unrecognized until it's too late to fix them.

With this multilevel model, the detailed plans that change the most are the easiest to change: Simply move sticky notes around or re-sort the activity list. At the same time, the major milestones remain fixed in a visible location. If the team changes the schedule so much that they cannot meet a schedule requirement in the next tier up, they will discover it as soon as they adjust their plans. When low-level activities are broken into days, slippages and schedule risks have no place to hide.

TEAM-BASED PLANNING PROCESS

The engine that drives engagement with this planning process is team-based planning, where not only developers, but also marketing staff, designers, and production engineers directly participate to ensure cross-functional alignment. In Lean Scheduling, project managers are facilitators who help the group develop the project plan and keep it updated. The project manager is the expert on the company's product development process, but the team members are the experts on the work required to deliver the plan. The project manager does not own the plan—the team owns the plan.

The team builds the Level 1 plan at a kickoff workshop. The team brainstorms the list of decisions and then pares the total number down to the essentials. Then they identify the key knowledge that will be required to make decisions. Those items become the deliverables that the team will need to complete. Finally, the team creates a work breakdown structure that shows sequence, timing, and dependencies between deliverables and decisions. They optimize the plan and then review it at the major decision points along the way.

Even if the Level 1 plan will eventually be computerized, the group uses simple tools like magnets and sticky notes to build the Level 1 plan. This gives the team the ability to optimize the plan themselves, simply by moving pieces around. As a result, they walk out of the workshop with a deep understanding of the project plan and how it impacts them personally. The project manager must not change the plan on his or her own after the team has committed to it. If the project manager moves things around arbitrarily, it becomes the project manager's plan—not the team's plan.

At the same meeting, they will build their first Level 2 plan, showing the work for the next three months. The process is similar: Brainstorm the list of key decisions and deliverables that will be required in the next three months to meet all the deliverables and make all the decisions in the Level 1 plan and then organize them into a work breakdown structure. This plan will be reviewed and extended every month or every four weeks.

Unless the entire project team is smaller than 12 people, subteams build Level 3 plans for themselves to meet their Level 2 commitments. To help ensure that nothing gets missed, Suzanne encourages teams to define each Level 2 task on a simple A4 sheet that lists the Level 3 tasks that need to be done in order to fulfill the Level 2 task, along with the task owner. These Level 3 tasks get consolidated into the subteam's Level 3 plans. The Level 3 plan gets minor updates daily, with major updates when the Level 2 plan gets updated.

STATUS UPDATES

The biggest hurdle that Suzanne's organization has had to overcome is the discomfort that some engineers feel because their work is so visible.

Engineers in general don't like the feeling that their managers are looking over their shoulders all the time. On an overloaded team, visual planning is overwhelming because the overload is so visible, and yet the teams usually lack the power to change it.

Suzanne has found that teams feel more comfortable when they don't have to follow a standard process for their Level 3 plans. She has given them flexibility to use a number of different formats for their visual plans or activities lists. It's also important that tasks do not get imposed upon the engineers by an external planner—that the engineers themselves develop the plan. The project manager is successful in this environment to the extent that he or she can help resolve blocking issues, foster collaboration across teams, and identify problems early, while letting the teams solve problems themselves. A command-and-control manager is going to face a lot of resistance to visual planning because that management style does not create a safe environment for surfacing problems.

Frequent updates are also important because they help the individual engineers and teams recognize problems while they are small, and prevent surprises. Daily stand-up meetings, a key component of Agile Software Development, is the gold standard. This is a 15-minute meeting designed to answer three questions: What got done yesterday? What's going to get done today? What's in my way? When updates are this frequent, the engineers learn to recognize their true capacity for a day's work and to give better estimates for the time it takes to complete a task.

At first, most engineers recognize that they overestimate their capacity and underestimate their tasks. For a product development team that is frequently late and/or overworked in late development, this can be a depressing realization that will challenge the project manager's leadership skills. Everyone, from the senior leaders in product development to the newest engineer, needs to remember that the visual plans have simply made reality visible, where the problems can be fixed. Within a few cycles, their plans begin to improve, they see opportunities to eliminate some tasks that become unnecessary or to prevent problems, and they begin to see how visual planning makes them faster by helping them remove all the things that slow them down.

RESULTS AND NEXT STEPS

Suzanne and her team measure 12 aspects of project management to see if Lean Scheduling has improved the team's ability to manage product development programs. Surveys of team members and managers show that this method has given everyone a clearer view of the true status of product development programs, increased team involvement, and led to clearer decision making. Figure 9.3 shows how the percentage of milestones met versus milestones planned has significantly improved.

When I interviewed managers and product development team leaders at Philips about how this method had helped them, they frequently reported that Lean Scheduling had led to clear alignment within the team and increased transparency for stakeholders. Suzanne says, "Lean Scheduling has become the core of our Lean Product Development program, but it's important to remember that it is only one piece. The problems that the teams uncover in their planning become areas that we target for continuous improvement so that we can remove the barriers for everyone."

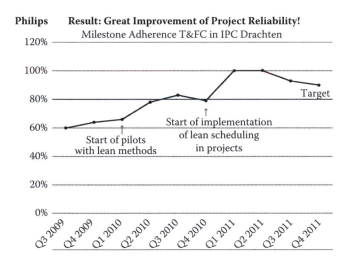

FIGURE 9.3
Improvement in schedule conformance at Philips.

Discussion Questions

- How do your group's project teams manage their schedules and budgets? How well is that working? How long does it take?
- If your company has software developers, do they use Agile Software Development practices? If they do, what results have they seen from these methods?
- How much time does it typically take to prepare for a status update, checkpoint, or gate meeting? How could you make the preparations for these meetings less labor intensive?

Next Actions

- ☐ Build a simple visual planning wall for yourself: tasks to do, tasks in progress, tasks complete. You can organize tasks by day or week.
- ☐ Set up a visual planning wall for your team, with at least two levels of schedule: immediate actions for the next two weeks and midterm deliverables for the next 90 days.
- ☐ Experiment with using a Status Report A3 instead of preparing a slideset to keep your stakeholders updated on your team's progress.

Section IV

Lean Product Development to Make Products Better, Faster, Cheaper

10

Novo Nordisk: Metrics to Drive Change

Novo Nordisk, a pharmaceutical company based near Copenhagen, serves a global population of 285 million people with diabetes, a number expected to double by 2030. According to the American Diabetes Association, in the United States, over 25 million people (8.3% of the population) have diabetes. The Centers for Disease Control reports that 1.9 million people were diagnosed with diabetes in the United States in 2010. By 2030, the number of diabetes patients worldwide is projected to exceed 400 million people. Diabetes is a chronic illness, and treatment options help patients control their blood sugar to prevent damage to the body's systems. This damage can cause blindness, heart disease, kidney failure, or amputation. In the United States, the total economic burden of diabetes in 2007 was US $174 billion. For a population this large, even a small improvement in disease management can add up to a large improvement in patient quality of life and in the lifetime cost of care.

At a presentation at the 2011 Lean Product and Process Development Exchange (LPPDE), Bella Englebach of Johnson & Johnson called drug development "the longest, costliest product development of them all." Drug development breaks down into roughly two stages: First, researchers identify a possible molecule to target a disease and then do everything possible to test and refine that molecule before it enters clinical trials. In the second phase, a series of clinical trials demonstrate the safety and efficacy of the drug. The chance that any given molecule will make it through clinical trials is less than 10%.

Tine Jørgensen, PhD, is the cLEAN® partner of Novo Nordisk's Diabetes Research Unit (DRU), assigned to work with the 700 diabetes researchers. The people she works with are pharmacologists, biologists, chemists, and experienced lab technicians—all leaders in their respective fields. This audience can be reluctant to accept ideas that come from

ABOUT NOVO NORDISK

Novo Nordisk has been a world leader in diabetes care since 1923, with leading positions in Hemophilia Growth Hormone Therapy, and Hormone Replacement Therapy. The company has more than 32,000 employees in 75 countries, who are all committed to delivering financial, environmental, and social results. Novo Nordisk invests over $1.7 billion per year in research and development.

other industries because their work is truly like no other product development process: A typical R & D process takes between 10 and 15 years and requires interaction with layers of customers (FDA, general practitioners, and specialists) before the product hits the end user. Tine says, "In order to get these people to accept and work with the ideas, you must show them how this will work, and involve them in the translation and interpretation. Just telling them is not enough. They need hard evidence from a comparable setting."

Yet the unpredictable nature of biological systems, the massive coordination with research programs and regulatory agencies, and the multidisciplinary collaboration make it difficult for Novo Nordisk's scientists to relate to examples from the automotive industry. The pharmaceutical R & D development model involves years of fast iterative optimization cycles to discover the one optimal development candidate, which then undergoes 8 to 10 years of safety and efficacy testing before submission for approval by the regulatory agencies. On the surface, this would seem to be nothing like automotive development. Given how expensive drug development is and how long it takes for a new drug to reach patients no matter how safe and effective it is, this is an industry that constantly needs to optimize its processes to increase value and reduce waste.

For Novo Nordisk, when Lean was initiated in the production area, it was imperative that the company define Lean for itself. Starting in 2006, a group within Novo Nordisk's DRU began exploring and developing cLEAN®, Novo Nordisk's internal interpretation of Lean, for use in diabetes research. By 2007, the group had begun to see some promising results. By 2011, cLEAN® was spread across the entire R & D organization.

cLEAN®: LEAN AT NOVO NORDISK

Novo Nordisk calls its internal Lean program "cLEAN®" and anchors it in the company's shared values around teamwork, respect, employee involvement, simplicity, and quality. The "c" in cLEAN® stands for "current" and it helps keep groups focused on leveraging their experiences—their current state—to develop new opportunities. The "c" helps make the connection to the pharmaceutical industry's quality system: "cGMP" means "good" manufacturing process inside Novo Nordisk. cLEAN® is a reminder to question everything and break down unnecessary barriers, while keeping the toolbox simple and the solutions local. Pharmaceutical companies tend to be bureaucratic, cautious, and slow—all attributes that lead to a lot of waste in internal processes. cLEAN® strives to help Novo Nordisk retain and strengthen its relative agility in this industry.

THE INTERPRETATION OF LEAN AT NOVO NORDISK R & D: SIX BASIC PRINCIPLES

The six principles of cLEAN® harken back to the basic principles of Lean Thinking, as Jim Womack articulated in his book, *Lean Thinking,* first published in 1998. Womack characterized the principles of Lean thinking as value, the value stream, flow, pull, and perfection. Novo Nordisk interpreted these principles for themselves and added one more (Figure 10.1):

- **Value/waste:** Understanding what value—and waste—look like in the context of pharmaceutical development. The sheer number of customers creates a complex picture of value: Patients, doctors, hospitals, national health services, insurance companies, and pharmacists all have differing views of value. While everyone wants to put the patients' needs first, there is a lot of disagreement about what the patients need the most. At the same time, an outsider would look at a process with a less than 10% success rate and claim that it must be inherently wasteful. Pharmaceutical companies recognize this and they rapidly adopt new methods of modeling and testing

The Six Basic Principles of cLEAN®

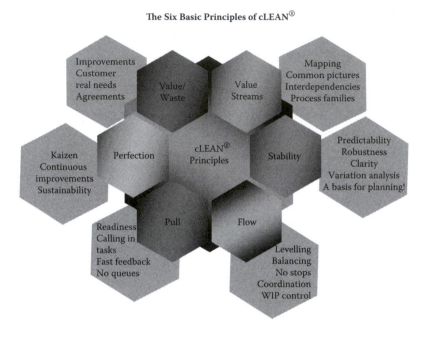

FIGURE 10.1
The Novo Nordisk cLEAN^O framework.

to screen out molecules before they reach clinical trials. At the same time, the best thing that a pharmaceutical company can do to increase chances of success is to increase throughput and capacity in the processes that are bottlenecks. It could be that the failure rate for preclinical testing may need to go up so that the number of successful drugs can increase. At the same time, it is equally important in the early phases to ensure optimal ideation and decision processes to make sure that the right things (drug candidates and projects) are pursued.

• **Value streams:** Visualizing the flow of value through pharmaceutical development, especially the interdependencies, so that everyone has a common picture of the process. The processes in a pharmaceutical company are inherently complex and heavily regulated. The teams working on drug development find that they get a lot of value from simply visualizing the processes in ways that help them to understand how the different parts of the organization work together. In such a large process, it is easy for people to focus on only their own work because the overall goal of the project is so uncertain and so distant. By making one person's part in the value stream clearer, it helps build stronger commitment to the goals of the overall program.

- **Stability:** Ensuring that processes are robust and predictable so that plans are reliable. This is especially important in a process that has so many dependencies among transactional processes. In this environment, fast is good, but it's better to be predictable than fast. At the same time, improvements in shared processes, such as the ones that coordinate clinical testing, are shared among all of the drug development programs, compounding their benefits.

- **Flow:** Balancing and controlling the work in process to avoid overloads and bottlenecks. This is the ability to understand the whole process and its subprocesses well enough to recognize bottlenecks and other flow problems, and then to put countermeasures in place to remove them. Drug development has the potential for transactional process flow problems that result in backlogs and long lead times, as well as knowledge flow blocks that make it more difficult to leverage the organization's knowledge among teams working on similar classes of molecules.

- **Pull:** Eliminating backlogs and ensuring that downstream teams are prepared when the time comes for them to take things into the next phase of development. This is also about ensuring that handoffs from one team to another work smoothly. Given how long this process is and how much of it is bound up in experiments that take time to perform, the teams don't have any time to waste on missed handoffs or bottlenecks. Pull is also the enabler of fast feedback ensuring that resources are being used on the right things—the best and most promising hypotheses, drug candidate series, and projects.

- **Perfection:** Committing to continuous improvement and sustainability. This is a common focus of Lean programs throughout the enterprise, but at Novo Nordisk, this is not just a slogan. It is the way that the company's Lean teams break down the massive work it would take to overhaul such a large process into smaller chunks, and then ensure that the changes stick after an improvement project is finished.

METRICS: A BALANCED VIEW OF
ORGANIZATIONAL PERFORMANCE

All product development organizations need a mechanism to assess their ability to meet their multifaceted mission of delivering value through new products. This is a distinct activity from the tactical measurements that a program manager must use to assess a specific program's performance against its objectives, schedule, and budget. Dave Packard, founder of HP, often said, "What gets measured gets done." Metrics focus a group's attention on the things that are most important to the company's leadership, and the right metrics drive progress toward achieving the organization's strategic objectives.

It is better to manage a critical few metrics than it is to create a complex set that requires a lot of time to collect, report, and interpret. From a Lean perspective, the time spent managing metrics is "necessary waste"—non-value-added activity that should be minimized. Each metric will need an owner who is responsible for collecting data and reporting the results.

MEASURING SUCCESS ACROSS PRODUCT
PROGRAMS AND TIME HORIZONS

In product development, we have two challenges to consider before defining metrics: variability across programs and lag time. Each product development program differs in the amount of technical and market risk, the effort required for completion, the amount of reusable knowledge that is available to the team, and the ease of integration into the organization's existing operations. When the goal is faster time to market, how does one measure across such wide variances in complexity?

We address this challenge by seeking out predictive metrics that are independent of the type of program. For example, we cannot meaningfully measure reduced cycle time across products unless we have many of them to smooth out the variation. We can measure estimated time between phase gates versus actual time. We can also measure actual time to market (often from concept approval to launch) for programs of similar size, scope, and risk. Some groups develop categories (research, breakthrough, platform extension, refresh) and others weight scope, technical risk, and market risk to create a sizing score (small, medium, large, very large).

Metrics for Measuring Financial Performance
- Expected ROI for the entire PD portfolio over three years
- Percent of revenue from new products per year
- Mean breakeven time for new products by program type

Metrics for Measuring Customer Value
- Number of returns, customer support calls, or warranty claims
- Customer loyalty or customer satisfaction survey data
- Number of voice of the customer/visit the customer gemba events (or number of employees who participated)

Metrics for Measuring Operations
- Development cost by program type
- Number of new products by program type released per year or product cycle
- Number of new products that hit their expected launch dates

Metrics for Measuring Learning and Growth
- Utilization of the organization's knowledge supermarkets: content growth, number of searches, usefulness of content
- Number of hours devoted to activities that deepen technical, process, or customer knowledge and then capture it for reuse
- Number of preventable rework cycles

TRANSACTIONAL VERSUS KNOWLEDGE CREATION PROCESSES

Novo Nordisk's product development process generates as much knowledge if not more than a typical product development process. However, drug development is also peppered from beginning to end with transactional processes that lend themselves to Lean Operations tools. Transactional processes have less variability and more repeatability than

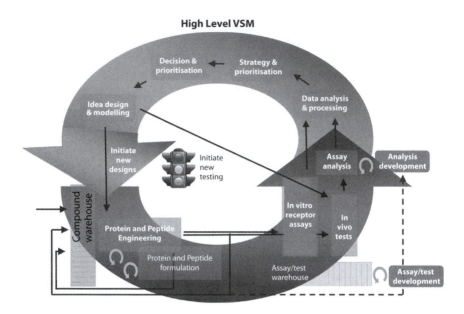

FIGURE 10.2
Novo Nordisk's High Level VSM of the Drug Development Process.

knowledge creation processes. For example, a standard toxicology test is a transactional process because there is not much variability in the activities performed to conduct the screening from sample to sample. In fact, the test needs to use standardized methods so that results can be compared across tests. The toxicology results, of course, may vary greatly, but they don't change the way the toxicology test is performed.

As a result, the DRU cLEAN® group at Novo Nordisk has used value stream mapping more extensively than any other case study in this book. Figure 10.2 shows their high-level value stream that describes the flow from creating- and management-driven activities in light gray to process-driven activities in black. They use value stream mapping to improve processes at every level. In one early pilot project on a common type of test activity, they were able to triple throughput of this process, which had become a bottleneck. At the same time, they have not ignored the knowledge creation side. State-of-the-art electronic lab notebooks and compound databases help make their reusable knowledge more accessible, while making it easier for Novo Nordisk to prepare patent applications, with much less waste.

CRITICAL QUESTIONS MAPPING

The other companies featured in this book have learned to identify and close their knowledge gaps early. In drug development, the sheer number of knowledge gaps for any given molecule would overwhelm any attempts to close them all. Critical question mapping helps to identify the most important knowledge gaps to close. In a presentation for LPPDE-NA 2011, Andrew Seddon described a critical question map as a tool to understand what subdecisions must be made, and in what order, so that a much larger decision can be made with confidence. It's like a project plan except that it shows the knowledge gaps that need to be closed instead of the activities that need to be done.

At Novo Nordisk, critical question mapping has helped teams delineate how to sequence the various model opportunities and experiments that could be done. The teams built a coherent strategy for how to get to the key knowledge about a molecule most efficiently before deciding whether or not to take it to the next level of investment. In some projects, it might be better for Novo Nordisk to identify and screen more compounds—and then kill them—before development enters the expensive clinical phases. Critical question mapping provides a concrete way for teams to uncover the questions they can answer early and cheaply that will help them find fundamental problems with a molecule as early as possible.

KEEPING PROGRESS VISIBLE: METRICS AND KPIS

An organization the size of Novo Nordisk relies heavily on metrics and KPIs (key performance indicators) to manage performance. For Lean to demonstrate its worth in such an environment, it must deliver measurable results. The DRU cLEAN® team has focused on how to ensure that progress with cLEAN® is sustainable by developing the right metrics to monitor.

An organization this size collects a lot of data, but only some of that data is readily available across enough programs that are worth turning into metrics. DRU has developed an internal system for tracking key process information such as the volume of work in progress, capacity, and throughput. That makes it easier for the managers to make better decisions about how to prioritize and allocate resources. It also provides the basis for an understanding of the impact that the cLEAN® activities have had on the organization as a whole.

Once the cLEAN® team knows what data are available in what formats, they are ready for a discussion with managers about which of these metrics will make the most sense for long-term engagement. The data are compiled into metrics, which get reviewed for completeness and accuracy. After that, managers set new targets for improvement. For example, a testing group could receive a target that they should increase throughput by 20% without adding additional personnel. These targets drive improvement activities.

Then, once a KPI has been met, it gets reviewed against the overall goals to make sure that the metric is driving the right improvement targets and behavior. Assuming that it is, the KPI becomes a trusted means to measure that cLEAN® is indeed doing what it says that it's going to do. It begins to develop true meaning. Essentially, this process of developing metrics supports rapid learning cycles, although "rapid" in this context is likely to be months instead of weeks or days.

RESULTS AND NEXT STEPS

Dr. Jacob Steen Petersen, corporate vice president of diabetes pharmacology and bioanalysis, Diabetes Research Unit, reflected on the last six years of working with cLEAN® in DRU:

> We have evaluated the impact of the overall benefits from all the individual cLEAN® projects, the KPI focus on predictability (speed and learning cycle turnaround) and the impact on quality through standardization and rapid learning. Today, we have faster access to relevant information, and also have higher data quality. They combine to give us the ability to make faster and better decisions, allow us to handle much more complex concepts and have increased our "innovation mass." Today, we run more projects faster and better. Our early project portfolio is larger, with higher quality projects and a more diverse risk profile.

Discussion Questions

- In your industry, what is the balance of knowledge-creating (innovative) versus transactional processes (verification testing, rote design)? Does your own PDP acknowledge the differences between these two activities?
- How long does it take for you to know whether or not a product was successful? How do you know? What measures are most important?
- How do you measure the health of your product development process?

Next Actions

- ☐ Create a definition for time to market and review projects for the past three years to see how long they took. You can place projects into complexity by category to recognize the differences between projects. What patterns do you see?
- ☐ If you use a phase gate product development process, do the same exercise to see how long it took teams to get from gate to gate. What patterns do you see?
- ☐ Lean out a transactional process: Make it easier to run a verification test, request a prototype part from the model shop, or get travel approval.

PRODUCT DEVELOPMENT CHECKLISTS AT UNGER

Company: Unger Marketing International, LLC, is a leading provider of innovative cleaning tools with about 10 design engineers working at facilities in the United States, Germany, and China.

Problem: Unger's former product development process would not scale up to deliver the number of new products that the company needed to meet its commitments to a major customer.

Countermeasure: The engineering staff developed a flexible checklist that incorporated everything the teams needed to deliver a new or modified product. Although the checklist is all inclusive, it is not restrictive. The team that is responsible for delivering a program is in charge of deciding the items that will be done—and the items that will not be done—for their program. As the team experimented with countermeasures for the problems they found in product development, they embedded that knowledge into the checklists. You can download a sample checklist on the sample documents and templates page at the Mastery of Innovation website.

Results: Cross-functional teams use the checklist today for all of Unger's products in every division, ensuring that the countermeasures that the team develops get used across all of its projects. As a result, the team was able to launch all of the products for its major customer on time—27 new products within 11 months. Paul Adams, vice president of R & D says, "The checklist worked for two reasons: First, the team that uses it owns it. Second, we can see that it helps us get better."

Next steps: The team continues to use the checklist as the basis for improving its product development value streams. Paul says, "As we keep finding ways to get better, we update the checklist to make sure that we use what we've learned."

Color Status / #	Milestone Sort	Task Items			
		Tasks (Milestones to be highlighted in light orange)	Dept. Resp.	Original Date of Completion	Planned/Actual Date of Completion/ Color Coding showing status
1	1	TG1		Enter Date	Enter Date
2	2	TG2 - Product Definition (Send PA To Controller)		Enter Date	Enter Date
3	3	Kick-off Meeting With Team	PM	Enter Date	Enter Date
4	4	Marketing Design Brief / Mis (Pro Only)	Mktg	Enter Date	Enter Date
5	9	VOC & Market Research (Why?)	Mktg		
6	10	Product Definition & Scope With Key End User Needs (In Market Brief)	Mktg		
7	13	Competitive Benchmarking	R&D		
8	14	Patent & Trademark Search	R&D		
9	15	Concept Development	R&D		
10	16	Confirm Technical Feasibility	R&D		
11	5	Complete Design Guide & Test Plan (With Quality) - Design Guide Must be Detailed To Prevent Misunderstanding	R&D	Enter Date	Enter Date
12	11	Go-n-see (End User / Usage / Facilities)	Mktg		
13	17	Review Books of Knowledge of Similar Products And Features	R&D		
14	22	Review Information on Similar Product Quality Data (Customer Returns, Quality Alerts, etc.)	Quality		
15	18	Determine All Areas That We Need to Test Prior to Starting Design	R&D		

A portion of Unger's checklist.

11

Visteon: Knowledge at the Engineer's Fingertips

For the past four years, Visteon's development group in Chelmsford, UK, has been part of a European Union project, named EU-FP7, to understand and apply Lean Product Development. Through that program, Visteon has leveraged the expertise of the research teams at Cranfield University's Lean Product and Process Development Group. The group's director, Dr. Ahmed Al-Ashaab, gave me a warm and enthusiastic introduction to Paul Ewers, the Continuous Improvement Manager for the Global Electronics Product Group.

Visteon was spun off from Ford Motor Company nearly 12 years ago and now develops components for most of the OEMs (original equipment manufacturers) in the auto industry. The Electronics Product Group develops the sophisticated electronics systems that control features like audio, instrumentation, displays, and control panels. Their vision is to "connect people to their vehicles and the world around them."

Since Visteon is in the automotive industry, it is no stranger to Lean initiatives. However, these have typically been more focused on the manufacturing plants. Paul says, "Over the years we have moved away from 'badging' things. We believe in stripping away all of the extraneous stuff and just incorporate the things that fit." Paul's group has benefited the most from books and presentations that have given him practical advice. The theoretical works have not appealed nearly as much. Visteon has two collaborative projects with Cranfield, which have focused on how to distribute knowledge for design decisions and set-based concurrent engineering.

ABOUT VISTEON

Visteon is the leading provider of value-added components and systems to a diverse set of global automotive OEMs, with 26,500 employees in over 26 countries. The company delivers climate management, electronics, interiors, and lighting systems designed by over 3,000 engineers in 24 global technical facilities. Its goal is to be the best in the world at partnering with its customers to provide innovative high-quality products that deliver exceptional value. The website is http://visteon.com.

LEAN PRODUCT DEVELOPMENT AT VISTEON

Visteon's Lean product development program has two objectives:

- Develop products that can be manufactured in a Lean production environment.
- Develop products in a Lean way.

Paul's own background includes a heavy emphasis on Six Sigma. At first, his team tried to use DMAIC, Six Sigma's primary problem-solving method, to help them figure out how to accomplish these objectives.

When companies have a Six Sigma initiative, the Black Belts (Six Sigma-certified improvement project leaders) from the corporate Six Sigma program may be "helicoptered" in to run projects and then leave. As soon as they do, people begin to revert back to their old ways of doing things. This was not the case at Visteon. The Black Belts were integrated into the product development organization and led improvement projects in their business areas to drive management accountability for results.

However, even with buy-in from the business and a standardized high-level process, DMAIC projects often attempted to standardize lower levels of the development life cycle. Yet high variability at these lower execution levels can make it difficult to use historical measurement data. This variability, compounded with the long lead times associated with product development, meant the DMAIC projects in product development often ran out of steam before they reached the "improve" or "control" stages.

SIMPLE PROCESS MODELS

In 2006, Paul got everyone from the leaders to the engineers engaged in developing a set of detailed process models. The engineers used the models to improve their own work. Their models fill in the details that would be too cumbersome to incorporate and standardize at the higher levels of the process. Since the engineers were the ones running the projects, they owned the initiative themselves. That made it easier for everyone to own the future states, too.

Since these models would be used to identify and implement improvement actions, it was important to document what people actually did. This required buy-in at all levels, since the reason why a process is not performed as originally intended may not be immediately obvious.

Value stream mapping is the most common tool used in Lean programs, but it has its challenges when used in product development. Visteon sidestepped these issues by using the "simple common language" developed by Nimbus Partners. This simply defines the activities, inputs, and outputs and clarifies who should perform the activities. This process helped Visteon build visual models of its processes that anyone could read and understand (Figure 11.1). Paul's group organized the maps into a three-level process architecture: high-level corporate product development process, intermediate level variations to meet specific regional or product segment

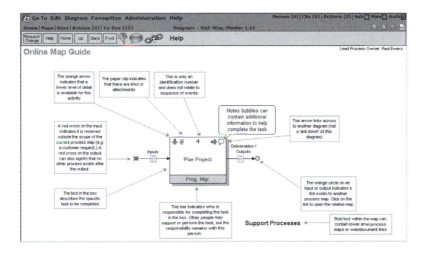

FIGURE 11.1
Visteon's project map.

requirements, and the low-level processes that took place within engineering disciplines.

As the teams built their future-state maps, they recognized the need to integrate with their OEM partners' product development processes and embedded sufficient flexibility to accommodate partner requirements. At the same time, they leveraged what they could from the Capability Maturity Model Integrated (CMMI), a model used to assess the process discipline of development teams.

It was a lengthy process—two years from the start of the mapping process until the documentation was good enough to use. After the new process had stabilized, they trained auditors to ensure compliance with the process. They believe that this has improved delivery performance by ensuring that the project's deliverables get met. But just as Paul challenged the corporate model for Six Sigma, he also challenged the idea of having outside auditors.

LEAN PROCESS AUDITS

Paul strongly believes that processes must be owned and managed by the people doing the work, and Lean manufacturing experts see inspections or audits as waste. Yet Visteon is a complex organization with demanding customers, and the different engineering disciplines rely upon standardized processes to help them manage this complexity. Visteon uses a network of auditors to ensure compliance with the process and to identify any problems with the process or barriers to compliance.

In the traditional view, auditors come in from the outside. These auditors may be more impartial but they usually lack sufficient knowledge about detailed product development activities to understand what they see. Paul has found a way to balance the engineers' need for process ownership and flexibility with the corporation's need for standardization and verification, while ensuring that the information generated through the audits gets used for continuous improvement. The first step was to identify a network of embedded auditors who are more familiar with the work being audited, but are not so close that they have a direct stake in the audit results. This makes it much more likely that the information generated through the audit will reflect customer and business value, and that the process problems get fixed at the appropriate level in the company.

To help his network of auditors, Paul developed an automated system of storyboards and reports to guide embedded auditors through the process of conducting an audit to determine process compliance. These tools make it easier to delegate responsibility to the engineering disciplines while providing consistency in data reporting. The audits are limited in scope to keep them fast, light, and useful.

He was able to increase audit coverage without increasing the number of people involved in auditing. Most important, auditors within engineering disciplines have much more credibility with the engineers than a group of outside auditors, as well as much greater ability to recognize when the process is the problem, rather than lack of compliance.

The audits provide the raw data to guide the group's continuous process improvement. By focusing on what they already do, identifying the gaps, and then carefully selecting countermeasures, Paul believes that Visteon has found the right balance between process discipline, to avoid the wastes of reinvention, and flexibility, to give product development teams the right tools at the right time.

REUSABLE KNOWLEDGE

If Visteon had simply continued to improve its product development process using Lean methods, the company would have eliminated enough waste to make all of its efforts worth the investment. Yet I have seen a lot of organizations go through all of this, only to have their efforts fall apart because the process cannot adapt to new challenges in product development. However, Visteon took its process maps to an entirely new level by linking the organization's critical knowledge directly to the processes that the engineers use to do their work.

Visteon has put all of its reusable knowledge and process documentation into a web-based tool that links it directly to its current state process models. A person can go to the step in the process that describes where he or she is and the tool will link him or her to everything that needs to get done. By doing so, he or she has reduced the time it takes to access this key information from 17 minutes to under 40 seconds. When the cost savings were added up across all of Visteon's engineers, the IT system more than paid for itself.

WHEN TO USE PROCESS MAPPING IN PRODUCT DEVELOPMENT

The companies in this book have taken a wide variety of approaches to process mapping in product development. Some groups have used value stream mapping or some other process mapping methodology extensively. Some have used it, but abandoned it because it did not address their core problems. Others have deliberately left it alone.

Here are some questions to ask to decide whether or not process mapping will help your company:

- How formal and complicated is the current state of our product development process? Would a mapping session help us understand where we have problems with handoffs or give us ideas about how to remove some of the complexity? Or would it just add complexity to a process that is working well enough?
- Do we suspect that our product development process is overloaded with excessive documentation, long approval cycles, status reporting, or functional silos? Would a process map make these problems more visible?
- Have we already identified and addressed the sources of waste in product development that are common across organizations, such as scatter, late manufacturing involvement, late customer feedback, insufficient knowledge transfer across programs, and unproductive meetings, if they apply to us?
- Is the Lean Product Development transformation likely to change the product development framework dramatically as teams spend more time on knowledge creation, knowledge capture, and reuse, with less time on detailed design? Will doing a framework-level process map at this time support or inhibit this change?
- What is the current state of our product development framework? What does it contain (common milestones, document templates, checklists, etc.)? How effectively do the product development teams use it today? Is it seen as a mandate, a set of guidelines, or something in between? What are we prepared to do to ensure that the improvements identified by the

framework-level process map propagate to all of the product teams?

- Have we identified a specific purpose for this process mapping session: streamline decision making, improved handoffs, eliminating procurement-related delays, etc.?
- Is the process to be mapped on the critical path for product development? If not, then what are the benefits of streamlining it?
- Are we prepared to follow through with the work required to move from our current state to a future state product development process? We may need to rewrite documentation, update templates, retrain the development teams, or negotiate agreements with partner organizations.

These days, most large organizations have an internal website with the company's product development process (PDP). The PDP site usually contains templates, checklists, and example documents that program managers use to fulfill the requirements of the process and prepare for management reviews. The problem with most PDP sites is that it's not easy to find the most important things. They quickly get cluttered with documentation that represents attempts to avoid missed handoffs between groups. These PDP sites can be so difficult to navigate that program managers abandon them.

At the same time, the sheer number of items on a checklist can be overwhelming when the checklist is all batched together under one management review milestone or one checkpoint meeting.

Paul and his team solved this problem by using their set of process maps as a starting point to build a visual system for knowledge sharing and reuse. The process maps serve as the organizing principle for the group's reusable knowledge. Most PDP sites present information as lists grouped under large phases of development. Visteon's system goes far beyond this to link templates, examples, and other reusable knowledge to the specific point in the process where it will be used. By representing the process visually, it's easier to find the right materials at the right time and easier to judge whether or not a particular piece of knowledge, a template, or a recommendation applies to a specific project.

RESULTS AND NEXT STEPS

The process models have now created a stable foundation on which to implement some of the deliverables from the collaborative Lean Product and Process Development Project. Visteon's next steps are to work with the Lean PPD Consortium to broaden its Lean Product Development program in these directions:

- **Lean measurement:** The group is exploring ways that teams can integrate process measures into product development projects so that improvement teams can use project data to assess the performance of the product development process. Visual management tools make these process measures visible within the different levels of the organization.
- **PD value mapping:** This is a new mapping tool to assist process analysis by providing an integrated view into waste and value to quantify the level of improvement that this kind of process analysis can yield.
- **Set-based concurrent engineering (SBCE):** The group will pilot SBCE for a specific project and compare results to those from similar projects that used traditional engineering methods.

Discussion Questions

- How long does it take you to find knowledge and information within your company? What are the barriers that make knowledge and information hard to find?
- Has anyone in your group ever tried to map the product development process? What happened?
- When you capture a piece of reusable knowledge (an A3 or a simulation model), where do you put it today?

Next Actions

- ☐ Make a list of the systems that store knowledge and information that you access freely. How well are they integrated?
- ☐ Track how much time you spend in a week to hunt down the information you need to do your work. What are the big areas that waste the most time?
- ☐ If you have no collaboration tool like SharePoint, create a simple file share where people can begin placing their reusable knowledge.

A KNOWLEDGE-BASED FRAMEWORK TO SUPPORT PRODUCT DEVELOPMENT AT METSEC PLC

Company: Metsec PLC in Oldsbury, West Midlands, UK, is an innovator in the cold roll forming industry. Cold roll forming is a means of forming flat metal strips into things like railings, beams, and metal framing. The company's largest market is the building and construction industry.

Problem: Metsec is in a traditional industry, with some long-term markets in decline. It needs to replace those lost customers with new ones in growing markets, and to capture market share from competitors with higher quality standards, faster turnaround on custom work, and cost effectiveness. Traditionally, Metsec approached product development with a customer order in hand and short lead times. Engineers would start designing products and tooling quickly and then fix problems later with postproduction design changes. This made the cost of quality unacceptably high.

Countermeasure: Alan Harris, Quality Manager at Metsec PLC, became convinced that Metsec needed better ways to access the knowledge the company had developed about cold roll forming processes, and to put that knowledge to work for new customers. Alan used process mapping to help Metsec's engineers understand what areas of knowledge were most important and then gave them some simple tools to help them capture that knowledge. Then he built a manufacturing knowledge base and product data archive to make it easier to retrieve the organization's knowledge.

Results: Alan admits that implementing this system wasn't easy. He says, "The implementation was strewn with difficulties, both culturally and practically." His main challenge was to get the engineers to document their problems and provide their knowledge in ways that all people involved in product development could understand and use.

Alan describes two types of benefits from this system. First, there has been significant improvement in quality, cost, and delivery metrics. Quality levels improved by 56% in three years and the cost of correcting problems dropped by 84.5%. While Alan admits that the company's program to replace obsolete equipment has driven some of these gains, it's clear that Lean Product Development has made it much easier for the engineers to deliver products that work well the first time the production department runs them.

The intangible benefits include a much deeper understanding of Metsec's manufacturing capabilities and development processes. Alan says, "The system has not replaced the user's ability to determine the necessary actions to be taken; it has acted as a tool to supply the information and knowledge needed."

12

A-dec: Project Chiefs to Speed Decision Making

A-dec is a small, family-owned company based in Newburg, Oregon, that produces dental equipment and furniture for the global market. Early on, A-dec made the key strategic decision to develop a business that could be sustained in the face of pressure to outsource and reduce the quality of its products. Lean Manufacturing has played a key role in helping the company fulfill that strategy while still delivering products that have high value in the marketplace. A-dec now sees that its product development system is key to fueling the company's long-term growth.

The Chief Engineer is one of the most intriguing aspects of the Toyota Product Development System. As described in the literature, the Chief Engineer, or *Shusa*, as they say inside Toyota, is the person directly responsible for integrating customer, technical, and process knowledge into a new product. Toyota's Shusas are legendary for their ability to develop and drive the vision for a new car.

Like many entrepreneurial founders, Ken Austin served as the company's Chief Engineer for many, many years. This should be no surprise: Entrepreneurs often succeed because they deeply understand a specific customer group well enough to design unique products to solve that customer's most important problems. If they had not deeply understood their customers and their products' technology, they would never have built successful companies.

At the same time, every founder reaches a point where it is time to turn product leadership over to others so that the founder can focus on the company's strategic growth. Even though it has been a long time since Ken has been directly involved in product development, Phil Westover, a Product Chief, says that stepping into Ken's shoes has been a big job.

ABOUT A-DEC

As the world's leading manufacturer of dental chairs, delivery systems, and dental lights, A-dec provides reliable dental equipment solutions to better the lives of dentists and their patients worldwide. The 50-acre A-dec campus in Newberg, Oregon, includes state-of-the-art manufacturing facilities and labs for engineers and product designers. The company's website is http://a-dec.com.

LEAN PRODUCT DEVELOPMENT AT A-DEC

A-dec began moving Lean into product development about three years ago. Like other companies in this book, it used book studies to help it gain a basic understanding of the theoretical underpinnings of Lean Product Development. Then the product development leaders collaborated on the creation of a future state product development system that distilled the elements of Lean Product Development that seemed to have the greatest potential for A-dec, and they showed how these practices would integrate with A-dec's corporate vision, mission, and values.

For these leaders, Lean Product Development is the means to ensure that the company is sustainable over many years as a family-owned, family-oriented business with tremendous respect for people. A-dec's business is built around maximizing flow in its customers' value streams. The only way to be that kind of business in today's global market is to have world-class products that dentists will buy because they make their work easier and better, even if there are cheaper alternatives.

The future state details A-dec's ultimate goals for Lean Product Development, and the company will move toward this future state step by step. A-dec decided to begin in an unusual way: by reinventing how product development program teams were managed. In most Lean Product Development organizations that I've seen, program leaders' roles evolve as the company learns about Lean, but it takes a long time for the program leader position itself to change. A-dec decided to move immediately toward a new model for product development program leadership.

FIRST STEP: TEAM LEADERSHIP

First, A-dec tried a hybrid option that called for a team of three managers to serve as joint product development program leaders. The three people came from three different functional areas. Each manager was responsible for making decisions in his or her own area, and the team made decisions jointly that cut across all of the functional areas.

I have seen this model work at other companies, as an interim step to build experience when there is no one who has all of the customer, technical, and process knowledge to lead a product development program, but it requires the three managers to sit in the same area, spend most of their time together, and commit to making rapid decisions. The product program leadership team also needs a strong commitment from senior management to avoid interference, no matter how tempting. A team of two or three seems to attract more of this micromanagement than single program owners do.

At A-dec, this model broke down because no one was accountable. The group was slow to make decisions, and projects got slowed down in general. Fortunately, they recognized that they already had the people inside the company who could take full ownership for their most important product development programs.

THE PROJECT CHIEF

Phil Westover is the Project Chief responsible for the dental treatment room furniture lines. A-dec's Project Chief role is inspired by the literature on Toyota's Chief Engineer, heavily adapted to fit A-dec's specific needs. Although he has some experience with woodworking, he is not an engineer; his background is in HR, and then Marketing. This may surprise some people, who take the term "Chief Engineer" literally. In practice, this role needs to be filled by the person who has the deepest understanding of customer and business value, along with the technical mastery to develop innovative solutions. That person may not be an engineer. I have seen industrial designers, chemists, food scientists, and even master perfumers play this role successfully.

INNOVATION MASTERS: LEAN PRODUCT DEVELOPMENT PROGRAM LEADERS

The Chief Engineer is a cornerstone of the Toyota Product Development System and one of the most difficult parts of Lean Product Development to execute outside Toyota. In fact, the term "Chief Engineer" is itself problematic. It's the term Toyota chose to replace *Shusa* or "Product Manager" in its own product development process. But other companies have Chief Engineers whose jobs have no resemblance to the shusas and in some Lean Product Development organizations, the real Chief Engineer is an industrial designer, a technically savvy marketing director, or even the company president. The question that matters is, "Who is ultimately accountable for creating the vision for this new product and then driving that vision to a completed product that a customer can buy?"

Today, I call these people "Innovation Masters"—because that's what they are. They are the members of the organization who have the greatest mastery of the company's technical knowledge, customer knowledge, market opportunities, and business needs. Innovation Masters are the people responsible for developing innovative product visions and then driving them toward conclusion. To do that, they need deep customer, technical, and process knowledge. They also need these personal characteristics:

- **Systems perspective:** Innovation Masters have the ability to see the entire product and its ecosystem, even when looking at only a small piece. They can make decisions that reflect their ultimate vision for the product even when the decisions themselves are small.
- **Customer empathy:** It's easy to develop the product we want to buy ourselves; it's harder to develop a great product for someone who has an entirely different set of abilities, interests, and needs. Innovation Masters have the ability to build an understanding of the customer's perspective and see customer needs that the customers themselves cannot articulate.
- **Convergence mind-set:** Innovation masters are comfortable with the uncertainty that is inherent to convergence. They have

the ability to delay decisions and to encourage others to delay them until the last responsible moment. They value the flexibility they gain from convergence and they recognize when it is time to converge so that the product program stays on track.

- **Stakeholder awareness:** Innovation Masters build strong relationships with the people who will be critical to the successful execution of their product vision. They take care to ensure that they have open lines of communication with partners, senior leaders, and other key stakeholders in the development process so that the organization can stay aligned as the product vision evolves.
- **Courage and conviction:** They develop bold product visions that push the organization's comfort zones and advocate successfully for their ideas. Once they have the go-ahead to execute the vision, they take responsibility for steering their vision through the development process, making tough decisions to get the best balance of customer and business value.

There is one thing that these people are not: project managers. From a Lean perspective, project management is waste—necessary waste, but still waste. These people have more important things to do than detailed budget and schedule management. They may need the help of a project manager so that they can focus on the value-added work of realizing the vision for a new product.

At A-dec, the engineering decisions are usually not that difficult, but the need to understand the customer and the customer's environment is paramount. The Project Chiefs are people who have demonstrated that they have a deep understanding of customer needs. The five Chiefs come from Product Management and serve as senior product managers. A few of them also have engineering backgrounds. An outbound marketing staff relieves them of most of the direct marketing work, like promotions.

In the past, the founder, Ken Austin, took full responsibility for all of A-dec's products. With this model, Ken has delegated that responsibility to the Project Chiefs, all of whom have worked at A-dec for long enough to understand how Ken thinks. As a result, the Project Chiefs and their teams feel much greater ownership for the success or failure of the product, and functional leaders support the Project Chiefs' decisions. Phil said, "I can comfortably take ownership and communicate the passion for what I'm trying to achieve with a product—I remind people that we own it."

Project Chiefs are accountable for success or failure of a product—especially those parameters that drive product acceptance in the market. They report directly to the Executive Committee and have all the authority they need to make market-driven decisions. As a result, the Project Chiefs don't get into the details of product design integration. Instead, they are responsible for leading voice-of-the-customer work and for making decisions about quality, aesthetics, and costs. Phil said, "The first projects using this model are about 18 months old, and so far, we've had no micromanagement—definitely pressure to reach our goals, but they seem to trust that we'll deal with the issues."

Engineering Manager Steve Peterson says, "This has been a really good thing for us. Our future state calls for even more strengthening of this role." At the same time, he recognizes that the company needs to learn what types of experiences prepare future Product Chiefs for this role, and then get more people in the pipeline.

PRODUCT DEVELOPMENT ORGANIZATIONAL STRUCTURE

While the Project Chiefs own their products, they use functional expertise in engineering and production to get their products to customers. Today, A-dec organizes product development using a matrix organization that resembles the way Toyota's Product Design Centers have been represented in the literature. This has helped the company strike a balance between the Project Chiefs' needs to deliver excellent products and the organization's need to improve the overall product development process and encourage knowledge reuse across products.

The functional departments own the knowledge and processes within their areas. Strong functional department managers are directly responsible for improving the processes that they run. The functional managers develop people and take ownership for building checklists and design guides, templates for standard deliverables, and knowledge capture. They take responsibility for ensuring that the knowledge gained in one product team gets transferred to other teams, avoiding the waste of reinvention.

The engineers see that the combination of strong functional managers with Project Chiefs has improved product leadership.

GO-AND-SEE CUSTOMER VISITS

A-dec has long recognized the importance of building deep customer knowledge around everything that happens in the dentist's office.

Dental furniture needs to be easy to clean and sanitize. A-dec asked Phil to tell the story of all the work they do to help dental offices eliminate the risk of infection. Over time, he created a network of people inside and outside A-dec to help the company understand infection control and then help dentists see the benefits.

To do that, Phil has spent a lot of time on go-and-see visits to dentists' offices, especially observing all the things that happen in between patients. Then he uses the information to create job maps to show what each person in the dental office does. Phil uses A-dec's customer list to find dentists willing to be observed. When he gets there, he just grabs a chair and sits in a corner, out of the way, watching everything. He shares everything he learns with everyone in the dentists' offices, who have often never looked at jobs from the perspective of flow, consistency, and predictability. Figure 12.1 shows how that translates into a system for streamlining sterilization by integrating it into the flow of the dental office.

For Phil, Lean is all about eliminating waste for his customers. He said, "My job is to eliminate hassles in the dental treatment environment, for the dentist, the hygienist, and the patient." Since people get accustomed to the hassles in their work environment, they sometimes have difficulty talking about how to improve a product to make it easier to use. The direct observations that Phil makes in his dental office visits helps him identify the hidden wastes that can lead to a product that feels a lot more comfortable, even if the users don't know why.

Phil also accompanies sales representatives on their visits. Here, Phil listens for the customer's perception of the product, especially around value and quality. A-dec has a good quality system, but in this environment, even a minor defect can become a major inconvenience or even a health hazard.

As the Project Chief, Phil has the ability to incorporate all of this knowledge directly into his products' designs so that the dentists and

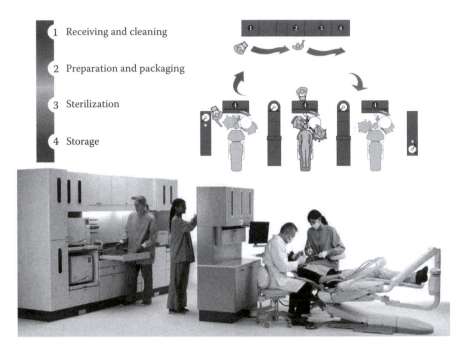

1 Receiving and cleaning

2 Preparation and packaging

3 Sterilization

4 Storage

FIGURE 12.1
A-Dec's Preference ICC Sterilization System.

hygienists enjoy working around A-dec's furniture. They find the furniture in the treatment rooms to be easy to maneuver around, convenient during patient sessions, and easy to clean afterward. The only way to identify the details that lead to such a positive experience is to uncover the environmental factors and inexpressible needs that one finds on go-and-see visits.

A-dec encourages everyone to go-and-see. Engineers accompany sales reps on customer visits, and technicians on service calls. In one instance, an engineer observed a technician as he performed some routine maintenance. The technician remarked on how useful a washer would be in a particular place. The engineer went back to the office and issued an engineering change order right away to add the washer. It's a small change, but for a busy technician, even a few minutes saved add up. These visits help tie together everything the engineer already knew about the product technology, the business goals, and the market needs by making everything more concrete.

RESULTS AND NEXT STEPS

Since A-dec named its first Project Chiefs, it has delivered more products with the same level of investment in new product development. By combining Project Chiefs with strong functional leadership, the company has developed a flexible process that is defined enough for appropriate knowledge sharing but flexible enough to accommodate all of the different types of products that A-dec produces.

From Phil's perspective, the company has moved forward both in product development effectiveness and in encouraging the growth of personal effectiveness, and he sees a lot of opportunity to leverage these benefits to help the company grow. Next, Phil intends to help A-dec do a better job with developing strategic plans and product road maps for his line of furniture.

Three years ago, he felt somewhat "been there—done that" about the idea of self-development. Now he's realized that he has to be on the lookout for self-development opportunities because he's never really going to "be there." A-dec has given him the role and the support to continue his personal path of mastery.

Discussion Questions

- What is the product development program leadership model for your group? Who is responsible for project management? Who has ultimate authority for technical decisions? Who is responsible for representing the customer's point of view?
- Who in your organization most resembles A-dec's Project Chiefs, Toyota's Chief Engineers, or the Innovation Masters described in this book?
- Who is ultimately accountable for the profit and loss performance of a product?

Next Actions

☐ Identify the areas where you already have the expertise of an Innovation Master, as well as the areas that are opportunities for growth. What can you do to grow into a position like this?

- [ ] Interview the person who is most responsible for a product development program in your group. Where does he or she see opportunities to improve the leadership model?
- [ ] Identify the key partner organizations who get involved in product development and the people that you know in each one. How can you expand your partner network?

Section V

Lean Product Development Transformation

13

Nielsen-Kellerman: Just Start Somewhere

Nielsen-Kellerman Company is very small. Its entire engineering staff consists of three people, led by their Engineering Manager, Michael Naughton. When I met Michael at the 2009 Lean Product & Process Development Exchange (LPPDE), he was new to Lean Thinking. His company had just embarked on its Lean journey, and Michael didn't know what that would mean for him and his team. I had the privilege of watching Michael and his team over the next three years as they sought to incorporate Lean Product Development ideas into their work in a way that was appropriate for them.

Nielsen-Kellerman has 90 employees and generated just over $12 million of revenue in 2010. They make handheld instruments for rowers and a few other devices that leverage the same core knowledge base. They have carved out a niche market that they own. With their size and scale, they simply don't need a lot of the structure that a larger product development organization needs. Everyone is all together in one place—most of them in the same room. They didn't need Chief Engineers, a documentation-heavy phase gate product development process, complex value stream maps, or sophisticated portfolio management tools. They needed to maximize value and eliminate waste.

Michael returned from LPPDE 2009 feeling a mixture of inspiration and frustration. He says, "I could see that it was possible to get much better performance from my team, but I didn't know what to do first, or how to use some of the tools I had seen, especially since the companies that presented were so much larger than NK." But he remembered that a speaker had said, "Just do SOMETHING different. It doesn't have to be perfect."

ABOUT NIELSEN-KELLERMAN COMPANY

Nielsen-Kellerman Company designs, manufactures, and distributes rugged, waterproof environmental and sports performance instruments for active lifestyles and technical applications, including Kestrel˚ pocket weather meters, NK electronics for rowing and paddling, and Blue Ocean˚ rugged microphones and PA systems. NK began business in 1978 in an upstate New York basement and remains committed to U.S. manufacturing to this day. Now located in Boothwyn, Pennsylvania, just south of Philadelphia, NK's team of 80 employees generates approximately $12 million in sales. The company's website is www.nkhome.com.

LEAN PRODUCT DEVELOPMENT AT NIELSEN-KELLERMAN

How does a company live into the spirit of Lean Product Development if none of the practices seem to apply? Systematic problem solving is the one practice that is universal. It is the practice that connects product development to the rest of the Lean Enterprise. For Michael and his team, Lean Product Development was simply the application of systematic problem solving to the problems that were right in front of them.

Michael began in the simplest way possible: observing the current state and reading about how others had solved the problems that he saw. Figure 13.1 shows the visual model that Michael created to capture the current state of product development at Nielsen-Kellerman in 2009. He found that his team typically had problems with projects that seemed to wander around from idea to idea before finding something that worked. Products took a long time and cost more than expected. The company lost sales and team members felt discouraged.

To bring his team on board, Michael facilitated a weekly book club to read Allen Ward's *Lean Product & Process Development* and asked the team to help him find the most important problems to solve first. They identified three places to start: inefficient meetings, the inability to capture and retrieve core knowledge, and the complete lack of a new product development process.

Then the team applied systematic problem solving to those problems. They specifically adopted the LAMDA cycle, the method that Allen Ward

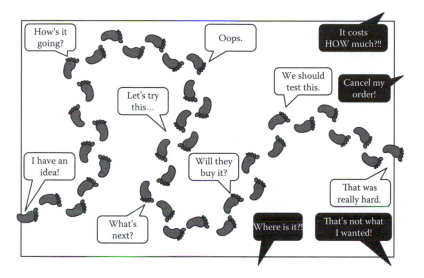

FIGURE 13.1
Product development at Nielsen-Kellerman in 2009.

developed to address directly the challenges of doing systematic problem solving in an engineering environment. LAMDA stands for LOOK–ASK–MODEL–DISCUSS–ACT. It encourages engineers to observe the current state of a problem for themselves (LOOK), identify root causes and reusable knowledge that may apply (ASK), create visual models to explain their observations and recommendations (MODEL), and get feedback on their ideas (DISCUSS) before they execute (ACT).

The team's solutions uncovered other problems. The team applied systematic problem solving to the new problems. Sometimes they were able to adopt ideas from larger companies and sometimes they just developed their own solutions. After three years, they had cut time to market more than half and positioned their company for its next growth phase.

INEFFICIENT MEETINGS: VISUAL PROJECT PLANNING

One advantage of such a small team is that they don't have the communication barriers that large companies have. All of the product developers are within 25 yards of each other, and the manufacturing facility is just down the hall. However, sometimes small teams take this free flow of communication for granted, and they don't develop an infrastructure that supports good project planning and tracking.

Prior to 2009, Nielsen-Kellerman's approach was the one most project managers take when they first recognize that they need a project plan. The project manager builds a project plan and then calls regular meetings for status updates. The product developers themselves contribute estimates to the plan but the project manager builds it: It's the manager's plan. The status meeting minutes get captured and distributed via e-mail, sometimes with updates to the project plan. The team's stakeholders get copies of the minutes, which they may or may not read. Minutes may be stored in a central repository, organized by meeting date, or they may simply reside in e-mail.

This approach is better than no plan at all, but it has some inherent problems. The plan is not the team's plan, and there is little individual ownership or accountability for the items on the plan. Action items from the meeting get buried in e-mail; if no one goes back to check, they get lost entirely. The review meetings themselves are focused around delivering status information to the project manager, instead of solving problems. Finally, typical methods for planning projects are too heavy for a team that is so small. The overhead of maintaining the project plan isn't worth it.

The team replaced review meetings and written status reports with visual planning boards. At Nielsen-Kellerman, the visual planning boards took the form of whiteboards with sticky notes and simple reports stuck to them. The sticky notes represented the activities that the team needed to complete so that the entire project would finish on time. The team worked together to populate these boards with project plans, and the result was a plan that the entire team understood, believed in, and committed to delivering. The physical act of moving, adding, and removing sticky notes for activities reinforces individual ownership for those activities. The new action items stayed visible throughout the week. Team members could check the visual planning board at any time to remember what they had committed to do.

When someone outside product development needed an update, Michael went up to the board and gave an on-the-spot project review that responded directly to the reviewer's questions. Once employees understood the board's layout, anyone in the company could update himself or herself by reading the board. Marketing and Production Managers could see that all of their pieces were in the plan, and they could watch the project progress week by week. This had two unexpected benefits: The entire company felt ownership for new products, and visual planning itself was contagious.

KNOWLEDGE CAPTURE AND RETRIEVAL: THE KNOWLEDGE LIBRARY

Next, the group tackled problems with documentation storage and retrieval. The group's core documentation was stored on individual hard drives rather than in shared systems. Not only did that make the group's knowledge difficult to find, but it was also not backed up reliably. NK was too small to have an IT department to ensure that things like backups got done. As the team dug into this problem, they realized how much time they wasted searching for information and how vulnerable they were to data loss.

The group held a two-day workshop to collect and organize core product knowledge onto a shared server and put some processes in place to maintain the knowledge library. The workshop included all of the engineers, plus key representatives from Sales and Marketing, Production, and Materials. By the end of the two days, all of the critical files had been moved into a central, accessible location and all of the workshop participants understood what this content was and how they should use it.

Through the discussions about how to organize core knowledge, the team developed a better understanding of how the organization fit together. They eliminated the time it used to take to search for information and to respond to information requests from team members. They made sure that all of their knowledge systems had reliable backup processes in place.

NIELSEN-KELLERMAN'S PRODUCT DEVELOPMENT PROCESS

After the first year, Michael repeated his assessment. He found that the early work had improved engineering productivity and knowledge sharing. They had eliminated some design loopbacks and were doing a better job with schedule predictability. But products still cost too much and

LAMDA: SYSTEMATIC PROBLEM SOLVING
FOR PRODUCT DEVELOPERS

PDCA is the most common systematic problem-solving method in Lean Thinking. PDCA stands for Plan–Do–Check–Act. When W. Edwards Deming went to Japan in the 1950s to teach operational excellence, he taught PDCA. Over the next 30 years, Toyota embedded PDCA into its management systems that became known as Lean. On its own, PDCA will not help a problem solver remember to define a good problem, to analyze the root causes, to consult stakeholders, and to think through the hypotheses that a Do step will test.

Allen Ward developed LAMDA in the early 2000s to address the problems with PDCA. LAMDA stands for LOOK–ACT–MODEL–DISCUSS–ACT:

LOOK: Go to the gemba. Go to the real place where you can see the problem for yourself. Get direct experience. Talk to the people who are closest to the problem. Make observations and consolidate them into a clear problem statement and a picture of the current state.

ASK: Ask two questions: "Why?" and "Who Knows?" The "Why" question will require at least some root cause analysis. The "Who Knows" question leads you to the experts—the people who have seen and solved this problem before. The answers to these questions deepen your understanding of the problem and begin to formulate your hypotheses.

MODEL: Use visual and physical models to facilitate your communication, document your observations, and develop your hypotheses. Most of the problems that product developers need to solve, both technical and organizational, benefit from the use of pictures, diagrams, sketches, physical prototypes, computational models, simulations, or other types of models.

DISCUSS: Throughout this process, you will have discussed your observations and analysis with others. In the DISCUSS step, make sure you have covered all your bases: Have you spoken with all of the stakeholders? Have you addressed the concerns of those who will be responsible for implementing the countermeasures? Who else do you need to talk with? What are the expected results, and do they justify the effort required to go into implementation? Finally, do you have a good implementation plan?

ACT: Execute the implementation plan and record results.

LOOK AGAIN: Look back on what happened. Did you get the results you expected? What do you need to do next? What have you learned? How can you capture it?

BENEFITS OF THE LAMDA CYCLE

The LAMDA cycle leverages the strengths we have as product developers. We instinctively go to the real place—the lab, the workshop, or the customer site—to learn about problems. We use models constantly, from data flow diagrams and object models to prototypes. We have an appreciation for the expert perspective. At the same time, it mitigates our weaknesses. We don't always take time to analyze root causes. Sometimes, we come up with a great idea and we just want to see IF it works; we don't want to take the time to understand WHY it works—or doesn't work. When we indulge that impulse, we lose our ability to develop solutions that we can leverage to solve more than one problem. We don't always remember to talk to everyone who has a stake in the decisions we make. LAMDA is the systematic problem solving method that works the way that product developers think.

The LAMDA cycle.

took too long to bring to market. Michael returned to LPPDE in 2010 with one of his team members to get some more inspiration and ideas, and they joined an online web class to learn more about the practices of Lean Product Development.

They learned about the importance of the appropriate amount of standardization and process discipline in product development. As a small company, Nielsen-Kellerman would never need the type of formal product development process that is critical for a company like Ford Motor Company or Philips Electronics. But they needed something that would help them ensure that they didn't miss any critical steps, they could capitalize on the knowledge built in previous programs, and they could continue to identify problems within product development to solve systematically.

At the same time, Nielsen-Kellerman was actively building Lean Thinking throughout the company. Other teams were removing waste by redesigning their own transactional processes that intersected with Engineering. Michael's team needed to build processes that connected with the value stream redesigns that were taking place in other parts of the business.

Over the next two months, they developed a standard yet flexible product development process that was appropriately scaled to their needs. The new process breaks the work down into phases, but allows for overlap between the phases so that work can get done when it makes the most sense to do it. The process standardizes the parts of the product development process, such as the interfaces with Marketing and Production, that are the same from project to project. At the same time, it explicitly provides time in early development for identifying and closing knowledge gaps, performing experiments to build trade-off curves that will guide decision making later in development, and working with Marketing to ensure that the engineers understand customer needs.

To improve the Engineering Team's interface with Marketing, both teams worked together to develop a Product Proposal A3 that captures all of the key information about a new product: customer needs, strategic alignment, technical risks, proposed schedule, and budget. They began working in cross-functional teams that managed themselves rather than relying on one project manager to coordinate all of the project schedules. They redesigned their development lab to bring the development teams into closer communication.

SYSTEMATIC PROBLEM SOLVING TO
SOLVE TECHNICAL PROBLEMS

At Nielsen-Kellerman, design loopbacks were a major problem. It took a long time to develop a full system prototype, and each prototype had too much untested design content with too many variables. As a result, new product designs took a long time to stabilize. Products didn't get out into the market on time, which made it difficult to time product launches to market needs. Product development costs were difficult to estimate and usually exceeded projections.

Early in their Lean Product Development work, they incorporated short, rapid learning cycles into the development process to develop and test subsystem components independently. They applied LAMDA to their product designs, as well as their process, to close their knowledge gaps as simply and rapidly as possible. After a year of experimenting with this approach, the team saw that they had the common tendency to rush into solutions, and that some problems seemed to return once they had been fixed. The team recognized that they had not always done all the steps of LAMDA well enough to prevent these problems.

This time, Michael read *Understanding A3 Thinking*, by Durward Sobek, to learn more about how to use systematic problem solving, and he shared what he learned with the team. In 2010, the group formally adopted a standard Problem Solving A3 template that reinforced LAMDA as their approach for solving problems. If someone skips a step while using this template, it's immediately visible to everyone else. By providing a good summary of the problem solver's observations, analysis, and recommendations, the A3 helps the entire team make better decisions. Once the problem is solved, the A3 provides a record of the group's solution that they can review later if the problem comes back or a similar one occurs.

As a result, they found that they solved problems more permanently and captured the knowledge they gained. They were able to see opportunities to solve related problems and eliminate unexpected waste. The template helped the group take a more disciplined approach to problem solving.

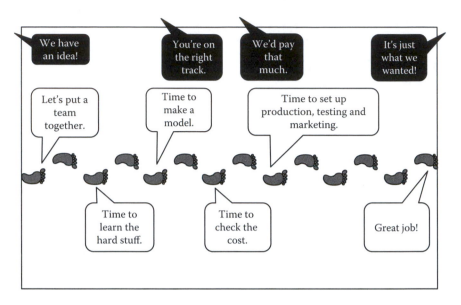

FIGURE 13.2
Product development at Nielsen-Kellerman in 2011.

RESULTS

Figure 13.2 shows the current state of product development in 2011. Michael estimates that each product is now more than $150,000 more profitable because it is getting to the market twice as fast. CEO Alix James says,

> Because we can count on a good flow of new products, we have been able to extend our company's leadership in its niches with products like the Kestrel 4400 Heat Stress Tracker for preventing heat exhaustion. We are also proud that we were named one of the top workplaces of 2012 in the Philadelphia area.

Discussion Questions

- How often do late design changes disrupt the development process and/or cause schedule delays? What are the major sources of these changes?
- How can you balance the need for clear product requirements and the need for flexibility to manage the unexpected in your product development programs?

- What systematic problem solving methods do people use inside your product development teams? What can you do to use them more effectively?

Next Actions

☐ Build a simple visual model that shows the current state of your product development process. This is not necessarily a process map; a conceptual model like Michael Naughton's can build alignment around the need to change.

☐ Review projects for the past two years to see if you can find any patterns that trigger late design changes. Does one part of your product fail at the end more frequently than others?

☐ Just start somewhere: Use LAMDA to solve a problem that maximizes value or eliminates waste.

BUILDING A LEAN CULTURE AT HIXSON, INC.

Company: Hixson, Inc., in Cincinnati, Ohio, is a leading architectural/engineering/interior design firm specializing in the design of R & D campuses, "good manufacturing practice" processing facilities for the food industry, corporate office environments, and retail centers for Fortune 500 clients across North America.

Problem: Although Hixson had been doing Lean for a while, they did not see individuals taking ownership for solving their own problems. Since the early 1990s, Hixson has practiced formalized Continuous Improvement (CI), driven from the officers at the top with firm-wide initiatives and department goals. The company has used hoshin planning, a Lean tool for setting and executing strategic objectives, to drive important improvements for over a decade. However, the leaders recognized that much of Lean's power is in individuals working to solve problems permanently in their daily work. It was as if the formal CI structure itself had become a deterrent to individual initiative.

Countermeasure: Hixson's officers made embedding Lean into their culture a top hoshin priority. They put in place a plan that included regular promotion of Lean concepts and "wins" at monthly all-company meetings, formal Lean initiatives focused on value stream mapping to identify and remove wastes from key processes, and formal study groups to help the company translate Lean concepts into a knowledge-based professional services work environment. Hixson also introduced training for all associates in the fundamentals of Lean Thinking and A3 problem solving with a "boot camp" approach that gave the associates lots of practice working on problems chosen by the associates themselves. The graduates from one boot camp became the coaches for the next, reinforcing the skills well after the formal class experience was over.

Results: By April of 2012, a critical mass of the firm's associates (70%) had participated in the A3 boot camp experience and learned systematic problem solving techniques. Lean Thinking and A3s have made their way into the common language of the firm. Associates are using these tools to accomplish specific improvements touching a wide range of work processes at a variety of levels.

Next steps: Beth Robinson, Director of Continuous Improvement says, "Moving an entire culture is like altering the direction of an aircraft carrier…it requires vision, persistence and time." Even though Hixson has made significant progress, the company feels there is still work to be done to make systematic problem solving second nature. Hixson plans to emphasize the role of management in encouraging and modeling A3 Thinking as part of each department's daily work. Beth says, "By teaching and coaching our staff members, our managers can create the 'pull' that will get the full capacity of the problem solving engine going. We believe this will get us to the next level and unleash the full power of *sustained* Lean results for the benefit of our firm and our clients."

14

Vaisala: From Pilot Projects to Global Transformation

Vaisala develops observation, measurement, and monitoring products and services for chosen weather-related and industrial markets. All Vaisala products need to be reliable, provide accurate measurements, and be operational in extreme conditions. Proven designs may stay in the market for years, and yet they must support both demanding industrial customers as well as researchers on the leading edge of science. These precision instruments look nothing like anything made by Toyota, but some of them may well be used in Toyota's streamlined manufacturing processes.

Jorrit De Groot, head of Operational Excellence during Vaisala's active Lean Product Development initiative, says,

> It was a huge shift for us to realize that the stuff in the Lean books was all about countermeasures…We have some of the same problems and some problems that are unique to us. Some countermeasures will work and others won't. We've used some Lean tools and we've developed some countermeasures on our own.

LEAN PRODUCT DEVELOPMENT AT VAISALA

Vaisala began its Lean Product Development work by chartering three pilot teams to experiment with the ideas in the context of real product development programs. These groups focused on developing visual planning boards to help them identify and track their knowledge gaps and to organize their work in the form of rapid learning cycles. A knowledge gap is anything that a product development team does

ABOUT VAISALA

Vaisala is a public corporation with €270 million in annual revenue (2011) and 1,400 employees worldwide. Approximately 20% of the personnel work in R & D and the annual R & D budget is around 10% of net sales. The company was founded by Dr. Vilho Väisälä in 1936 and is headquartered in Vantaa, Finland, outside Helsinki. Vaisala is a global leader in environmental and industrial measurement. Building on 75 years of experience, Vaisala contributes to a better quality of life by providing a comprehensive range of innovative observation and measurement products and services for chosen weather-related and industrial markets. The corporate website is http://www.vaisala.com.

not know yet, but needs to know in order to design a product. A rapid learning cycle is the method teams use to structure their systematic problem solving to close these knowledge gaps quickly. Each rapid learning cycle has a defined length, perhaps two or four weeks. During the rapid learning cycle, researchers try to close the knowledge gaps. At the end of that time, the researchers report their findings to the rest of the team.

The three pilot teams applied this approach to the early phases of their product development program. The results were promising enough that R & D leadership decided to immerse the rest of the organization in Lean practices. Their experiences proved that Vaisala's approach to Lean would be heavily focused on the need to surface problems and make them visible, and then to give teams the tools they needed to develop their own solutions to those problems.

The pilot projects gave Jorrit and the pilot teams the experience to figure out what Lean Product Development meant for Vaisala. Jorrit chose to adopt a simple definition: "everyone systematically solving problems permanently to maximize value and minimize waste across the organization." In practice, this means that every person inside Vaisala is responsible for solving problems within his or her own value streams to create maximum value for Vaisala as a whole.

While Vaisala would go on to adopt countermeasures from other Lean Product Development organizations, the most important changes have come from innovative countermeasures that Vaisala developed for itself.

VAISALA'S COUNTERMEASURE FOR
TRAVEL EXPENSE ALLOCATION

In the early days of Vaisala's Lean Product Development implementation, Jorrit gave the product development teams some basic information about Lean and encouraged experimentation.

Juha Nyman, Head of Device Platforms at the time, decided that he could eliminate the friction and delays in the way he approved the department's travel requests. His Product Managers traveled frequently to visit customers and attend trade shows. Each trip required his active review and approval. Some requests were routine, while others required follow-up with the Product Manager to learn why the trip was important.

Under Vaisala's system, his approval was necessary waste: It kept his department from depleting their travel funds too early in the budget period. Yet he recognized that he was not the person closest to the decision. His Product Managers were much better equipped than he was to evaluate the value of a given trip. But since they didn't know how much money they had to spend, they didn't have all the information they needed to make the decision.

Juha saw other teams experiment with visual planning as a way to coordinate the flow of work, and he wondered if he could use the same idea with his travel budget. He allocated his department's travel budget among the six Product Managers, and then he created a visual display on a whiteboard that showed how much budget there was and how much remained. He then told his Product Managers that he would automatically approve their requests as long as they agreed to stay within their travel budgets.

He noticed three things right away:

- Product Managers made much better decisions about which trips to schedule.
- The amount of time that he had to spend managing the travel budget went down significantly, freeing up his time for other things.
- This method provided a demonstration that visualization combined with respect for people could make a routine activity flow much more smoothly for everyone.

This may seem like a small problem to solve, but it was an important problem to the Product Managers. For the rest of the organization, it served as a powerful demonstration of Lean's potential to improve the everyday lives of the product developers. It is the kind of success that encourages others to lose their tolerance of the waste that surrounds them and to feel empowered to do something about it.

PRODUCT PORTFOLIO MANAGEMENT

A new approach to product development would not be possible if Vaisala's engineers were overloaded. Jorrit recognized early that R & D needed a better way to allocate resources to projects and to set reasonable expectations for Vaisala's business managers. To solve this problem, Jorrit worked with R & D and business managers to develop a visual portfolio planning system that makes the R & D organization's commitments visible to the entire leadership team.

The product development leadership team recognized that they had no good ways to manage R & D capacity. The leadership team used Excel spreadsheets to keep track of all the projects in R & D, but the spreadsheet was so complicated that a lot of key information was hard to see. The link between Vaisala's company strategy and product development was unclear, and detailed discussions about resource allocation did not clarify the connection. The sheer number of active projects made it difficult to evaluate them and budget for them effectively.

In 2010, Jorrit commandeered a hallway and covered it with whiteboards that he formatted into visual timelines. He printed out small magnets of "€10,000 bills" to represent the resources that the product development group had available and gave the "money" to business managers to "spend" on product development programs. Business managers could ask for more "money," but only if they agreed to contribute more real money to the R & D budget. They could not simply add more projects to the board without contributing the resources to support them.

Some fixed expenses, like support for current products, went on the board ahead of time, making it clear what resources were actually available to expend on new projects. The business managers then populated the rest of the board with the new product development programs that

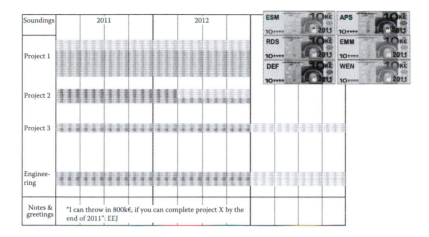

FIGURE 14.1
Vaisala's product portfolio planning board.

they wanted for the next planning cycle. When the board was full and the money was spent, there was no more room for other projects.

Figure 14.1 shows a diagram of the visual portfolio management board. It has a timescale of months running across the top, with spaces for projects in rows. Ongoing projects, maintenance, and overhead work are all preallocated at the bottom of the board. Space for new projects is at the top of the board. Vaisala has a series of these boards in a hallway where everyone in product development can see them. Everyone in the organization has a place to go to see what priorities the business managers have set.

The business managers populated the boards during a working session. In the past, they would have prioritized their projects on their spreadsheets, but then the spreadsheets would get filed away and no one would look at them. They were also infinitely expandable (there was no constraint on the number of projects the business managers could have) and too easy to change. As a result, it was easy for the engineering teams to be overloaded, and when priorities changed, some people didn't get the message.

The "money" is a key component of this system. It encouraged the business managers to take responsibility for how they spent the resources they had available to them. The amount of space on the board and the amount of money were both limited to match the true available capacity of the organization. This forced the conversations that needed to happen about how to prioritize the desired projects and how to decide which projects to kill.

It also makes the value of removing overhead visible, since that frees up "money" that the business teams can spend on additional product development programs. That has fueled the group's work to eliminate waste and speed up product development using other Lean practices.

The management team reviews this board on a quarterly basis. Jorrit has continued to refine the boards as the business managers learn more. They have a more accurate understanding of the overhead that it truly takes to run product development, for example. They have also experimented with different ways to load the work in product development to get maximum flow. The boards capture the prioritization in real time and that helps them ensure that everyone is in alignment around the strategic priorities.

The quality of the discussion about resource allocation was much richer and the decisions were much clearer than they were in the old spreadsheet-driven process. The psychological impact of spending money helped build strong leadership commitment for the projects on the board. The entire system made it clear which projects had the organization's focus and which ones did not.

In 2012, Jorrit planned to improve this system by using an iterative planning process that will reduce the effort required to populate the board. Projects that don't make the first cut won't need the same level of analysis as the ones that end up on the final board.

WIDESPREAD TRAINING

After a series of experiments like this over a year, Vaisala's senior leadership team made a commitment to extend Lean Product Development throughout R & D. Jorrit developed an internal training program that gave people the basic information and skills they needed. In 2011, he delivered it first to the management team and then to the entire product development organization. The training's core message: Lean Product Development for Vaisala is about finding problems and fixing them by developing countermeasures.

Most organizations design training programs to run for a few days, all in a row. Then people go back to their normal jobs and nothing changes. In a few weeks, without immediate opportunity to use the training and

THE POWER OF PURPOSEFUL PROBLEM SOLVING

Purpose is the reason why you need to solve a specific problem and how the solution will contribute customer or business value.

A good purpose statement creates a "value gap" between the current state and the future state that is compelling enough to get people to pay attention. Whenever you compare the situation now with a compelling future state, you create dynamic tension that pulls the problem toward resolution. Strong purpose statements reinforce this effect by making the value of the future state clearly visible. The more tangible and immediate the purpose is, the more pull there will be to get all the way through a learning cycle so that the value embedded in the purpose can be realized.

IS YOUR PROBLEM THE RIGHT PROBLEM TO SOLVE?

If it's hard to write a clear purpose statement, then you may be solving the wrong problem. Your problem may be too small or there may be other problems that are more important to solve. It's much better to find that out before you have invested significant effort in solving a problem.

Writing purpose statements requires personal honesty. No matter how important a problem is to you, you will not be able to overcome organizational momentum unless the solution has value to others. If you must make unrealistic stretches in order to demonstrate the value of the solution to a problem, then it is probably the wrong problem.

The process of writing a purpose statement tends to ferret out the problems that are solutions in disguise. If others don't share your appreciation for the value of solving a problem, then that may be because you have tried to sell them on a specific solution before you understand the problem well enough. It may be that the problem to solve is not the problem that is on the surface, and quick fixes rarely provide long-term value.

DRAW A "LINE OF SIGHT" FROM YOUR PROBLEM TO YOUR COMPANY'S NEEDS TO BUILD SUPPORT

Purpose statements draw a line of sight from your organization's most important objectives through to the specific problems that you solve on a daily basis. You may write all the Problem Solving A3s that you want on cost savings opportunities, but if the company is most concerned with speed to market, your purpose does not have strategic alignment and will probably not get very far.

It helps if you consciously speak the language of your company's strategic objectives: revenue, profit, ROI, growth, market share, cost, and speed are all goals that frequently end up in corporate strategy statements. Find out which ones have the most meaning to your decision makers by reading and listening.

When you reflect back the words that you see in your company's strategic plans, you make it easier for decision makers to see the connection between your problems—and, eventually, your recommended solutions—and the future direction of the company. That makes it easier for them to say, "Yes"—and mean it.

encouragement to try new tools, the learning dissipates. Even people who participate in a Lean event where they actually improve an existing process don't usually remember it after the training is over. The countermeasure to this problem is to spread out the training and make sure that homework assignments encourage the participants to use the new practices in the context of their daily work.

Jorrit's training sessions ran weekly for two hours, for eight sessions. Each session drilled into a Lean practice that Vaisala had chosen to embrace. Along the way, the participants had homework assignments to exercise their systematic problem solving skills. This continuous flow of training helped the participants integrate the lessons learned into their daily work. By this time, Vaisala had a wealth of examples from its pilot teams and other experiments to keep the focus on Vaisala's approach to Lean Product Development.

Managers participated in the classes so that they would be prepared to serve as coaches for their teams' participants in the class. Over the first six months of 2011, all of Vaisala's product development managers went through this training course. When I visited Vaisala in May of 2011, I could see the effects: Visual knowledge was everywhere. Not only were the product portfolio boards being maintained, but visual planning itself had also spread throughout the organization. They were beginning to see widespread adoption of A3 reports as the primary communication tool within Vaisala.

For Vaisala, the mastery of innovation is the ability to apply systematic problem solving to the organization's most important problems. All employees within Vaisala's R & D organization are empowered to eliminate the wastes they see in product development and their products, and to do it regardless of whether the countermeasures they develop match anything else within Lean Product Development. They are free to experiment with new approaches, strengthening the ones that work and discarding the ones that don't. They learn more about their products and their processes from every experiment.

VAISALA'S NEXT STEPS

Jorrit De Groot's next assignment is to take his experience with R & D into the business side, helping Business Operations eliminate waste and maximize value. Meanwhile, R & D leaders have followed up the training by incorporating Lean Product Development metrics into the balanced scorecard that they use to monitor the health of R & D.

Discussion Questions

- Do you have a problem with overload? How many projects does the typical product developer have? How do project developers decide among competing priorities?
- How much power do you have to solve the problems that are right in front of you? Do you have the ability to solve problems within your span of control without anyone's approval?
- What innovative countermeasures has your group already developed?

Next Actions

- ☐ Make a problem visible: Create a visual display to support one of your processes, like the travel allocation board.
- ☐ If you are overloaded, notice this week how you make decisions about which tasks will get done. What does that tell you about sources of waste and opportunities to increase value?
- ☐ Mentor someone on your team in how to use LAMDA to write an A3, as soon as you have written three A3s yourself.

END-TO-END LEAN PRODUCT
DEVELOPMENT AT GOODYEAR

Company: Goodyear Tire and Rubber Company develops tires and tire materials in three Innovation Centers with over 1,400 product development professionals.

Problem: High competition and a diverse customer set lead to a combination of high complexity and high variability in the product development process.

Countermeasure: Goodyear's Lean Product Development team recognized that there was no one single approach to Lean Product Development that addressed all of the opportunities they had to eliminate waste and maximize value from end to end in product development. Norbert Majerus said, "The team spent six years developing and implementing a Lean Product Development approach that synthesized the best ideas from the different schools within Lean."

The team used a combination of value stream mapping, theory of constraints to help them identify bottlenecks and improve flow in the process, visual management, concurrent engineering, and delayed decision making. They tied it all together with a comprehensive training program that leads to Goodyear's Lean Product Development Certification, the only one of its kind that I have ever encountered.

Results: The team has demonstrated that Lean Product Development delivers faster, cheaper, better. They have seen product adjustments decline steadily since 2007. They are able to deliver more products to the market, which helped position them for a quick recovery in revenues after the recession of 2008. They now hit 95% of their schedule targets.

Next steps: Norbert says, "The culture change starts with the process design and training. It continues with doing, continuing to make it better, and continuing to learn." Goodyear's Lean Product Development system encourages teams to experiment with the process to find ways to make it even better.

15

Playworld Systems: How to Cut Time to Market in Half—Twice

Playworld Systems, Inc., has always prided itself on its ability to understand the competing needs of the customers it serves. When the Great Recession of 2008 hit full force, Lean Product Development gave this family-oriented business the ability to thrive when others struggled.

Playworld makes commercial playground equipment for schools, new housing developments, and parks. Its sales were closely tied to credit markets, school board and local government budgets, and new home construction. When funding for these sources began to dry up, the commercial playground industry was in deep trouble.

But this company had some secret defenses. In 2003, the company began systematically to upgrade its operations to eliminate waste and streamline processes using Lean Manufacturing. By 2005, it had cut the time to fulfill orders from 10 weeks to nine days, and it had improved order accuracy from 85% to 97%. By 2005, the company began to reap the benefits of these efforts: less cash tied up in inventory, lower costs overall, lower costs to correct mistakes in customer orders, and more rapid response to changes in customer demand. Playworld began to move Lean practices into other areas of the business.

By the fall of 2008, the company set aggressive targets to make similar improvements in product development: shorten time to market from 18+ months to less than a year, ensure that all products hit their cost targets and launch dates, and reduce the hit on the factory from expedited prototypes to meet catalog deadlines. As the impact of the recession hit, the company began to appreciate the most important benefits of its program to reinvent itself: the ability to meet changing customer needs with flexibility and speed. Playworld had the ability to do things that its competitors simply could not do.

ABOUT PLAYWORLD SYSTEMS

Playworld Systems,® Inc., is a family-owned $60 million, 230-employee company headquartered in Lewisburg, Pennsylvania. Playworld Systems has been a leader in environmentally sensitive outdoor recreation and playground equipment for more than 30 years. Playworld Systems believes that "the world needs play" and brings fitness through play to people of every age through such innovative product lines as ENERGI˚, LifeTrail˚ Advanced, NEOS˚, PlayDesigns˚, Playworld˚, Activo˚, and Climbing Boulders™. The company's website is http://playworldsystems.com.

Despite 20% across-the-board cuts that hit product development severely, the company was able to get more products—and the right products—to market in the fall of 2009. Brett Barrick, Director of Product Development, shared the results:

> Ninety percent of our products were within 5% of their target cost and we got 50% more products out to the market than we had in previous years. We invested a 20% cut in R & D (research and development) expenses into more than 200% more tools to support new products. It was as if we got all the tools for free.

THE NEED FOR SPEED AND PREDICTABILITY

In 2005, Playworld Systems recognized that it had a problem turning ideas into products at a price that its customers would pay and within a time frame that would allow the company to meet competitive challenges. It took 18–24 months to develop a new piece for one of its existing playground systems. New playground systems took much longer.

The company's process for deciding which products got built was based upon "pretty pictures"—concept sketches the industrial designers created to describe their ideas for new products. While the designers knew enough about engineering and manufacturing to get a sense of how standard line additions would work, the process broke down whenever they tried to do something new.

Anything more than the simplest product line addition was plagued with design loopbacks and revisited decisions that delayed product launches from one year to the next. Products that appeared in the catalog might not be available until many months into the catalog year. Some new products were plagued with quality problems in the first months after introduction due to inadequate time for field testing.

Playworld often found that new products were much more expensive to produce than forecast, and that customers were not willing to purchase new products at a price that was profitable for the company. With all the investment in new tools already made, the company's sales and marketing department would have to find ways to justify a higher price.

Results from new product development efforts were disappointing. It took a lot of work to deliver a product that did not deliver the promise embedded in the "pretty pictures" seen so many months before, and products took a long time to develop traction with customers.

FIRST ATTEMPTS WITH LEAN THINKING IN PRODUCT DEVELOPMENT

Playworld decided to bring Lean Thinking into product development. The company sought to replicate the gains achieved in manufacturing upstream in engineering and design. When it made its first attempts in 2007, Lean Product Development was still new and not well understood. Like many others, Playworld first tried to use Lean Manufacturing tools like value stream mapping in product development.

These methods did not work. For one thing, most product development waste is invisible; it sits in hard drives or inside the overloaded brains of overscheduled engineers. The most important wastes in product development are the inability to deliver products at costs that reflect true customer value, ineffective decision making that leads to confusion, and the lack of systems to understand and capture the knowledge created in the product development process. That type of waste does not show up until the consequences are severe: uncontrolled rework loops that lead to product delays and, in the worst case, the inability to get the product shipped.

Doing a value stream map on a product development process that is too slow and costs too much is like mapping the process flow of a manufacturing process when an oil leak is creating a hazard. Most Lean

Manufacturing experts would agree that the priority should be the leaky, hazardous machine. The team should use Lean problem solving methods to fix the leak permanently and remove the hazard before trying to redesign the entire process.

In product development, **hazardous waste** is any activity that leads to unnecessary friction and frustration in an environment where the technical challenges are hard enough on their own. It causes teams to get bogged down in late development, release products months later than forecast, and disappoint the rest of the business. In the worst cases, product development can grind to a halt, while years go by with no successful product releases. Functional groups point fingers at each other to assign blame for product failures. Senior leaders may lose faith in their engineers and conclude that their company is incapable of innovation or that that there is nothing left to invent.

The typical product development group has "leaky machines" all over the place that generate hazardous waste. Every unproductive meeting steals time away from value-creating development work. Every revisited decision makes it harder for people to focus and increases the risks of miscommunication. Every time an engineer has to make a decision under pressure to make it work, without the time to make it work well, customer value suffers and product costs suffer as well. When it's easier to reinvent something than it is to reuse something that works, the organization misses opportunities to make things easier for downstream partners—all the way to the end user: a parent pushing a child on a swing.

A Lean Product Development organization eliminates these sources of hazardous waste, one by one, to free up time, energy, and money for work that directly contributes to new product development.

LEAN PRODUCT DEVELOPMENT AT PLAYWORLD

Playworld Systems' leadership decided to focus on eliminating wastes by improving their understanding of their production process as well as their ability to make effective product decisions for driving maximum customer value.

First, they put in place an A3-driven product definition process that helped them define each new product idea at increasing levels of refinement,

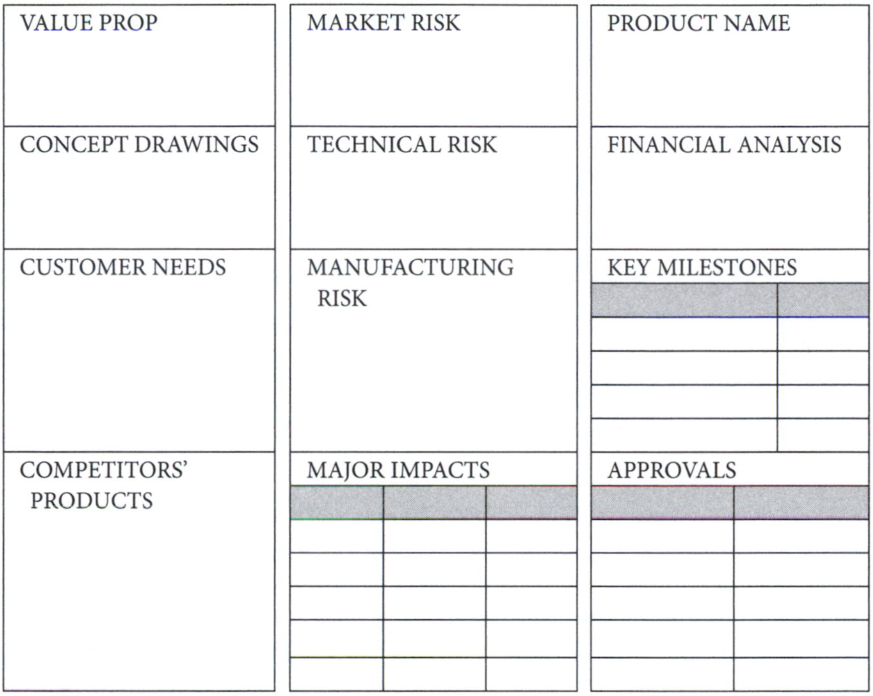

VALUE PROP	MARKET RISK	PRODUCT NAME
CONCEPT DRAWINGS	TECHNICAL RISK	FINANCIAL ANALYSIS
CUSTOMER NEEDS	MANUFACTURING RISK	KEY MILESTONES
COMPETITORS' PRODUCTS	MAJOR IMPACTS	APPROVALS

FIGURE 15.1
Playworld Systems' Product Definition A3.

capturing the history of key decisions. Alongside the "pretty pictures" of a new product, the industrial design team now had places to document customer needs, revenue forecasts, potential manufacturing issues, and unproven technology. That documentation keeps customer needs and target costs visible.

The resulting Product Definition A3 reports (Figure 15.1) drove good decision making through the boxes on the form and the approvals required. Playworld's template for the Product Definition A3 report created space for early input from the key functional areas that would be required to develop the product. This helped ensure that Manufacturing, Engineering, Marketing, Finance, and Industrial Design all delivered the information needed to make a good decision that stuck, without cluttering the product definition with extraneous stuff that they didn't need.

Second, they developed better ways to forecast product cost and then ran every potential product through the cost forecast model. That process helped the team get a sense of ROI (return on investment) for the product and gave the leadership team better information for making product concept decisions.

They defined more products than they needed. In Lean Product Development, pursuing multiple alternatives stimulates learning that a team needs before committing with confidence to a design. They capture the knowledge created through this process, and product concepts that don't make it into development can be revisited at a later time. The products that make it through this process have been more thoroughly vetted and are much more likely to be developed without expensive design loopbacks.

Then the team used visual management techniques to help them view the company's entire portfolio of products. They turned one large wall into the "Product Planning Wall," with each product represented on an A3 report. A limited amount of space on the wall corresponds to the organization's development capacity. That helps prevent overload and confusion about what products the group has decided to do. With industrial designers on staff, visual models were already an important part of communication at Playworld; the company's Lean efforts made them ubiquitous. In addition to the portfolio, visual planning walls track engineering tasks, schedules, and other commitments.

CUTTING TIME TO MARKET IN HALF—TWICE

Playworld Systems no longer wastes design resources on products that it will have to abandon. Good ideas get a fair amount of investigation when it's cheap and easy to explore them. Once an idea's contribution to customer and business value has been analyzed, then it goes forward or gets killed. The company can balance the mix of products based on better estimates of complexity, risk, and profitability.

The implications of Playworld's customer-focused Lean Product Development process for the organization are significant. In the midst of the recession, with 20% fewer resources, the company's associates delivered more new products—90% of them within target cost goals. They delivered those products in time to prevent most of the expediting that plagued prior years' catalog development.

Customers who see these products at the industry's major trade shows can order the new products with confidence. The products have all of the

TARGET COSTING

Target costing is an approach to managing product costs and gross margins that works backward from the price a customer will pay for a specific product with a specific feature set, sets product cost targets based on that product's expected gross margin, and then manages the development process to achieve the targets. This is different from how many companies approach product costs, where the teams may set targets based on historical data and prediction, and then set the price by adding a specific percentage of margin.

Target costing places customer value at the center of the financial decisions that a development team makes about a product. To do this effectively, a team needs to know such things as how much extra a customer will pay for a specific feature or level of performance, which areas of the product may be overperforming or especially difficult to manufacture, how to rethink a product design to make it easier and less expensive to produce, and how to partner with suppliers to drive down costs. The idea is to rethink our assumptions about a product and ask our customers directly to give us guidance on the elements of the product that create the most value for them so that we can deliver them more effectively and eliminate everything else.

The main benefit of this approach is increased gross margins, primarily by reducing direct labor and material costs for the product. One design goal can be fewer parts, which leads to savings in inventory management throughout the supply chain. The same techniques usually lead to products that are easier to transition to manufacturing, more reliable, and easier to maintain, which also drives down development, warranty, service, and support costs.

Surprisingly, this approach can make customers happier, too. By simplifying the products to reduce excess features and complexity, we can make the products easier to use and maintain from the customers' perspectives. They also benefit from lower service and support costs, as well as higher reliability.

TARGET COSTING TOOLKIT

This is a complex problem that encompasses the entire life cycle of a product, from concept to launch. A comprehensive toolkit for managing product costs includes some elements of the following:

- A portfolio management system to ensure that we are working on the right products with the right value propositions.
- Effective means to gather and analyze customer feedback, including opportunities to "go-and-see" for senior members of the engineering staff.
- Ways to identify the relative value of specific features and performance parameters, such as conjoint analysis.
- Methods for assigning priority to specific features and specs for a specific product at a specific price point.
- Models for predicting costs at the product and subsystem levels.
- Monitoring tools to monitor product costs continuously as the product moves through development.
- Platform development practices to leverage subsystem and part designs across multiple products to lower costs throughout the value stream.
- Value engineering tools to identify opportunities and implement strategies for cost reduction in the product design.
- Supplier management skills for bringing suppliers into the cost discussion as partners.
- Design for manufacturability and assembly methods and means for getting early feedback from production to lower manufacturing costs.

innovative design, quality, and safety features that Playworld has always delivered, at a price more in line with customers' expectations.

It is a little too early to say what impact this has had on sales revenue and Playworld Systems' bottom line. There are some promising early signs. The company's products stack up remarkably well against its competitors' products in trade shows.

Playworld saw a 29% increase in new products for its 2011 catalog over its 2010 catalog. At the same time, Playworld reduced the number of late projects by 29%, and only 1% of its new products were delayed more than

60 days from their scheduled introduction date. Playworld's new product introductions of 2011 were 138% higher (more than DOUBLE!) than those of 2008, which was the last year prior to Playworld's implementation of Lean Product Development techniques.

WHAT'S NEXT FOR PLAYWORLD?

In 2010, the housing construction and municipal budgets were still under serious pressure. To help these customers and to open up new markets, Playworld decided to put everything it had learned about Lean into a low-cost line of products. In the fall of 2010, the company launched a focused program to develop a new playground system from the ground up that is 40% significantly less expensive than its standard lines with equivalent play value.

This goal drove Playworld associates to challenge traditional assumptions about manufacturing and construction methods for playground systems. They used all of the skills they had built over the past two years:

- They pursued multiple alternatives to solve challenges in optimizing speed and cost.
- They built a simple visual planning wall in a corner of a conference area to keep track of major tasks, issues, investigations, and alternatives.
- They leveraged new knowledge and analytical methods to lower costs in their standard product lines and found ways to save cost on the value line, and they got everyone—Industrial Design, Manufacturing, Engineering, Finance, and Marketing—involved early in the product development cycle so that they could make robust decisions quickly.

The project team's experiences during the past two years gave them unshakeable confidence that they could meet this challenge. They delivered the entire new system—from idea to first commercial product sale—in less than six months.

Steve Malriat, chief operating officer, says, "Our next challenge is to learn from this experience to break free of the annual cycle. That will help us make the most of our organization's capacity and be even more responsive to customer needs."

Discussion Questions

- How well can you model the cost of a product? What are some of the major drivers of cost overruns for your products?
- How well do you understand your company's production capability? How well do you understand your suppliers' capabilities?
- How many new product concepts does your group evaluate to launch one product development program? What if you could evaluate twice as many?

Next Actions

- ☐ Visit one of your company's manufacturing facilities—ideally, one that makes a product that you helped design. If you can't do that, take a local factory tour.
- ☐ Interview an engineer at one of your company's key suppliers (you may need to invite a procurement person to participate in order to get approval). Ask what he or she knows about the limits of his or her company's systems.
- ☐ Convert a feature definition or product concept definition document into an A3. What are the most essential elements?

Section VI

The Path of Innovation Mastery

16

The Path of Mastery: How to Begin with Lean Product Development

I hope the stories in this book have inspired you to try out some Lean ideas in your product development teams. In this chapter, I will give you a road map to a Lean Product Development transformation. In my research, I learned that there are five stages to a Lean transformation (Figure 16.1).

Not every company goes through all five stages, although all of them go through the stages in the same order. Some small companies can move almost immediately into system-wide Lean simply because the system is so small. Some large companies may need to do focused projects to solve system-wide projects long after the rest of the transformation is complete.

HOW LONG WILL IT TAKE?

There is no simple answer to the question, "How long will it take?" but I can provide some general guidance to help you set expectations with others.

First, if you set up the Lean program with focused objectives connected to increased value or reduced waste, then you should begin seeing tangible results in six months: A pilot team will have reduced technical risk or a knowledge sharing system should have begun to generate reusable knowledge. If you have been doing Lean Product Development for more than six months and have yet to see results, chances are that your Lean programs need to be more focused.

Second, at least for the first three years, the results from these focused pilot programs and system improvement projects begin to reinforce each other. My own rule of thumb is that a pilot team doing Lean Product Development for the first time in an organization will be 30% faster—if

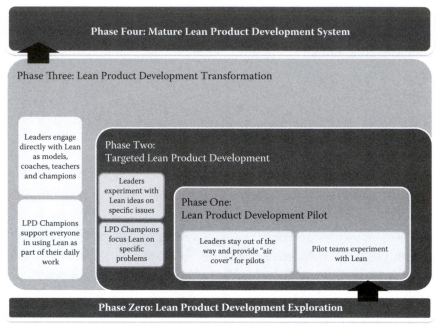

FIGURE 16.1
The phases of a Lean Transformation.

speed is what they care about—than similar projects within the same organization. The second team will be at least 50% faster as they take advantage of the first team's experience.

Third, the entire journey does take a long time. The companies that I believe to have mature Lean Product Development organizations have all been doing Lean Product Development for at least five years, and sometimes much longer than that. In fact, the mature companies I found (Scania, DJO, Novo Nordisk, and Goodyear) all believe that they still have a lot of room for ongoing improvement. They understand that they will never truly arrive at a final destination.

Finally, the speed of transformation depends upon your ability to pull these practices through the organization, rather than push them. A "burning platform" helps generate pull: a competitor who is outpacing you, dropping market share, lowered profitability, or a product that failed in the market. On the positive side, a technological breakthrough that you want to get into the market quickly or a new market opportunity can also generate strong pull. These situations shake people out of their complacency, creating space for new behavioral norms and beliefs. That makes it easier to pull Lean practices through.

THE PHASES OF LEAN TRANSFORMATION

Figure 16.1 shows that Phases 1–3 are nested: As companies move from Phase 1 (Pilot Programs) into Phases 2 (Targeted Lean) and 3 (Lean Transformation), they continue to run pilot programs and conduct focused Lean improvement projects. In fact, even mature Lean companies still engage in the activities in these phases to help them solve specific problems.

Phase 0: Exploration

Question to answer: What is Lean Product Development?

Challenges to overcome: Finding time to read, research, and experiment outside an official program, and building a community of people who are interested in exploring the ideas.

Pitfall to avoid: Buying into one author's or consultant's version of Lean too quickly without understanding the entire landscape of Lean Product Development, and expecting others to arrive quickly at the same place in the same amount of time that you have; selling specific Lean practices rather than focusing on how Lean can help solve the organization's problems.

Lean Product Development often begins when some product developer or product development leader reads a book like this one and gets inspired to try something new. Then the developer will seek out more information, reading a lot of things over a few months to begin to understand the lay of the land. He or she may conduct some personal experiments with Lean practices—for example, writing an A3 to solve a problem or setting up a personal visual planning system.

Then these explorers begin to get other people interested. They buy books by the carton and pass them around, invite an expert to give an introduction to the topic, send out links to resources online, and build internal presentations to make the case for bringing Lean into their organizations.

The biggest failure mode at this stage is to make presentations that "sell" Lean practices to people who have never heard of Lean before. Instead, practice your systematic problem solving skills: Look to find your most important problems; ask yourself and others if Lean can help you solve those problems. Build a model that shows how you would experiment to confirm your hypotheses about the problem and solutions and discuss it to get buy-in from influential stakeholders before making a high-stakes presentation to an executive.

Phase 1: The Lean Pilot

Question to answer: Can Lean Product Development help US solve OUR problems?

Challenges to overcome: Skepticism, poor understanding of Lean Thinking, overly aggressive schedules.

Pitfall to avoid: Overgeneralizing to the whole, based upon the success or failure of a small group. Pilot teams sometimes fail because the Lean tools were poorly executed, and sometimes they fail for reasons outside the team's control. Similarly, pilot teams sometimes succeed because they had leadership attention and priority standing.

In the Pilot Phase, one or a few teams use Lean practices to see what happens. A plant may 5S one supply area or streamline one production line. An accounts payable group might hold a kaizen event to redesign their workflow. In product development, one product development team will build their program around recognizing and closing knowledge gaps. By the end of this phase, the group should have gained some experience with Lean methods and have some evidence that Lean methods do make a difference.

A pilot project is the first attempt to use a new process, tool, or practice. We usually set up pilot projects when we already have a good idea that the new countermeasures are the ones we want everyone to use, but we recognize that we haven't fully worked out all the details about how to do it. The pilot project demonstrates that the new countermeasure will deliver the results that we need, with the opportunity to make adjustments as the new tools bump up against the reality of product development in our organization.

Pilot projects are more successful when we acknowledge from the beginning that they have two objectives:

- They must get their work done: deliver the new program, get the product out.
- They must adequately test the new countermeasure.

If it becomes clear that we cannot meet both sets of objectives, we need to make this visible and get alignment from our stakeholders before we take action or we risk killing the countermeasure. The way out of this dilemma is to charter the teams explicitly to deliver both the product and the process. If something outside the team's control makes one of these objectives impossible, they go back to their managers and renegotiate before they make the change.

The temptation sometimes is to select a small project as a pilot. Instead, I challenge you to think about piloting new countermeasures on your largest, highest stake, most important projects. Why? They are more visible, and there is more pull for them to succeed. That makes it easier to break down the barriers to a new approach.

If you truly believe that your new countermeasures reflect your current best understanding about how to deliver projects, why should your most important projects be forced to use methods that you know don't work?

With small projects, the biggest risk is that no one will care. When a countermeasure runs into unexpected problems and needs adjustment, it may not be worth the bother. Low-priority projects may simply not get enough management attention to demonstrate effectively that a countermeasure works, and if the countermeasure fails, the project may simply fail, too.

With a high-profile pilot, everyone in the organization has a stake in the success of the program. It is much more likely that the extra attention will make it easier to identify problems with countermeasures early, which is exactly what we want a pilot team to do. A problem is just something to fix, not a failure. When the pilot team succeeds, the countermeasures benefit from the visibility.

The biggest failure mode in this phase is to ignore the need for ALL of the pilot team's objectives to be visible and renegotiated when circumstances change. You don't want your Lean program to be seen as a failure because your pilot team ran into something that was outside their control. If you promise to be 30% faster but then discover that your supply chain partners selected a supplier that simply cannot meet the new deadlines, then others may say that Lean doesn't work.

In this phase, a leader's main role is to give the pilot teams the space to solve new things and help them work in new ways with partners as needed.

HOW TO LAUNCH AND SUPPORT A PILOT PROJECT

HOW TO KICK OFF A PILOT PROJECT

A pilot team benefits more than most from a kickoff meeting to get everyone in the same room to hash out the program details:

- All project teams need a clear target and objectives. This is even more critical for a pilot team because it has two sets of objectives. A pilot team's kickoff needs to make both of these objective sets explicit, with mechanisms for negotiating changes if needed.
- The team needs to know what success looks like and how the countermeasure will be assessed during and after the project.
- The team needs to understand how to adapt the countermeasure to their situation and how to improve it. If it's a new process, the deliverables must still be flexible. If it's a new piece of software, some provision needs to be made for development work to adapt the software to the needs of the team as they emerge. If the countermeasure is very hard to change, the pilot team may rapidly lose enthusiasm as they shake out all the improvement opportunities but cannot do anything about them. The pilot team itself may conclude that the countermeasure is a hassle.
- The pilot team will also need training and support to use the new countermeasure. Training alone is not enough because the countermeasure is not fully tested and will probably need at least a little tweaking. The kickoff meeting is an opportunity to begin training and skill development, and the team benefits from the shared experience of doing the training together.
- Finally, the team that developed the countermeasure—if this was not the pilot team itself—needs to ensure that the pilot team understands enough about the thought process behind the new approach. They need to know what problem the countermeasure is trying to solve and what benefits they will see from the improvement.

SUPPORT AND KNOWLEDGE CAPTURE FOR PILOT TEAMS

A pilot team's extra effort to test out a new countermeasure is waste if the knowledge they create is not captured. The team's own project documentation generally does not capture knowledge about the countermeasures they are testing. Lessons learned don't usually get captured until the project is over. At the same time, the team needs some support to build skills and adapt the countermeasure to fit the team's problems.

Ideally, someone from the team that developed the countermeasure works with the pilot team to help them build new skills, mentor them on using new methods, and fix problems as they occur. This person takes responsibility for the rapid learning cycles that will strengthen the countermeasure being tested. He or she is also responsible for capturing the knowledge that the team develops about the countermeasures in real time.

The team's mentor makes sure that the templates, document formats, process steps, etc. stay in sync with the countermeasure as it is actually being used by the team. Process maps, especially, tend to become obsolete as soon as they encounter the real world. The person assigned to support the team needs to take ownership for keeping them up to date. Someone also needs to convert the project team's documents into templates that other teams may use.

If the countermeasure delivers good results, chances are that others will want to leverage those materials even before the pilot team is finished. That is a clear sign that the pilot team has achieved all of its objectives.

Phase 2: Targeted Lean

Question to answer: What are our most pressing system problems, and how can Lean help us solve them?

Challenges to overcome: The fear of exposure, organizational inertia, leaders' resistance to changing themselves.

Pitfall to avoid: Delegating the problems—and solution development—away from the people doing the work. Leaders need to work on leadership problems like portfolio management; others cannot solve those problems for the leaders. Product developers need to work on product development problems; leaders cannot solve those problems for the developers. Operators solve problems at the operator level, and so on. Experts, even Lean experts, can facilitate and mentor but never do the work itself.

This is the phase where a group decides what Lean means—for them. This is where the specific elements of Lean will be tested and adapted to fit the group's environment. Building off the experiences of the pilot teams, the group tackles its most pressing problems using Lean ideas. In product development, they may realign the product development process to eliminate waste and excessive documentation, develop a product strategy and portfolio management process, and improve its ability to work with partners in Marketing, Supply Chain, and Production. In this phase, support groups such as prototype shops and test labs will start holding regular kaizen events and standardize on a system of visual management. Product development teams will pilot new practices such as knowledge capture and reuse.

The biggest failure mode for this phase is to fail to follow through on the actions that come out of problem-solving workshops. A workshop is just a big source of waste if people are not able to finish what they have started. Each workshop should have a focused objective and target, as well as the support to make sure that the workshop team can do the work to meet their objectives after they go back to their day jobs.

The product development leadership team gets actively engaged at this point to use Lean practices to solve their own system-level problems. By working on solving the problems that are right in front of them—without solving problems that belong to their teams—they build the problem solving skills and ability to recognize waste that will prepare them for the transformation. At this point, it is especially important for the members of the organization to see their leaders learning by doing. By the end of this phase, the leadership team should have direct experience with Lean and the confidence to move into a full-scale transformation.

Phase 3: Lean Transformation

Question to answer: How do we develop everyone into Lean Thinkers so that Lean is the default operating system for the group?

Challenges to overcome: "Flavor of the month" skepticism, legacy performance management practices, organizational scatter.

Pitfall to avoid: Aggressive rollouts that lack sufficient support structures. Training is not enough; people need access to mentors and managers who will hold them accountable for HOW they do things as well as WHAT they achieve, and who will actively clear away the barriers to Lean Thinking and systematic problem solving.

Now the group has clearly demonstrated success, and the leadership team has both the confidence and the experience to lead a Lean Transformation. This is the time to develop training experiences and align performance measures to nurture a culture of systematic problem solving.

The full-scale transformations that I have seen usually have these four components (Figure 16.2):

- **Training:** It is unreasonable to expect people to use systematic problem solving if they have never been expected to do it. Even though most engineers and scientists have been trained in the scientific method and may use it daily to solve technical problems, few have used systematic problem solving to eliminate waste and maximize value. Training helps close the gap and ensures that the organization has a common vocabulary for its own set of Lean practices, the forms of waste that it recognizes, and the value that is most important.
- **Direct application:** I know from experience that a person usually needs to write about three A3s to feel comfortable using the tool in a variety of situations. People usually write their first A3 in training but they then need immediate opportunities to create their second

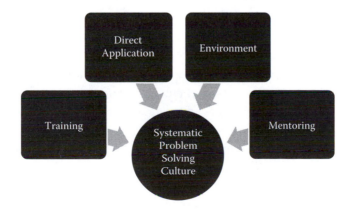

FIGURE 16.2
Support for a Lean Transformation.

and third ones. There is no point in introducing a Lean practice such as visual management to a group if they have no opportunity to use it right away. All transformation plans need to answer the question, "How do we get people using Lean practices as soon as they have finished training?" One countermeasure to this is to have new product development teams go through training together as part of their project team kickoff.

- **Mentoring:** This is the toughest problem to solve in an organization that is new to Lean: Who mentors the mentors? Fortunately, you probably built up a community of people in phases 1 and 2 who can help: All those pilot team participants and focused Lean problem solvers have experience with Lean tools that you can leverage. Mentoring is mostly about the ability to ask good questions. It is OK to carry around a list of mentoring questions to ask until they come naturally.
- **Environmental support:** The organizational models and management systems inside conventionally managed companies actively dissuade people from using systematic problem solving, and they generate a lot of waste that is obvious to people on the ground. Performance management systems may reward firefighting, rushing to solution, and accomplishing objectives at any cost. Those systems need to be dismantled and rebuilt to support the Lean Product Development system. Both formal leaders and informal leaders need to be especially careful about the examples that they set and the intangible rewards that they unconsciously pass out when they show admiration for a team's work. If you recognize firefighters, you will get fires.

The biggest failure mode in this phase is for leaders to see Lean as a spectator sport. The leaders need to make sure that they are walking the talk: solving problems systematically themselves and asking others to solve problems systematically. They need to make sure that they are supporting people who make problems and wastes visible rather than hiding them. They need to empower the members of their organization who are closest to a problem to solve the problem within clear parameters but without second-guessing. They need to hold people accountable for HOW they do things (using systematic problem solving) as well as WHAT they achieve.

Since the group solved systematic problems in phase 2, Lean has already helped everyone, making it easier to get people to try new things. Leaders will spend most of their time in this phase developing their people into Lean leaders.

Phase 4: Mature Lean Product Development System

Question to answer: How do we keep what we've built after all the easy problems have been solved, and how do we leverage our new capabilities?

Challenges to overcome: Complacency, fatigue, the counterintuitive nature of Lean practices, and on-ramp experiences for new employees.

Pitfalls to avoid: Bringing in new people, especially new mid- to senior-level leaders, who do not share the organization's history and experience with Lean practices and do not believe that it is important to maintain; growing so rapidly that new employees don't have enough mentoring to integrate into the Lean system; believing that the journey is ever finished, and that all the problems have been solved.

The companies that have been doing Lean Product Development long enough to have mature Lean Product Development systems have entirely different relationships with systematic problem solving, value, and waste than a company that is just starting out. They have moved into a place where Lean is part of the environment: People have internalized these concepts to the point that it is jarring when someone rushes to solution instead of asking "why" first. They have removed the most obvious forms of system-level waste, and knowledge has few impediments to flow.

The challenge here is how to keep Lean ideas fresh and alive when they are no longer new. The best way to do this is by continually raising the bar: It's great that we met our goals; now we need to be 10% better. The individuals who have been through a Lean transformation thrive on this kind of opportunity.

The biggest failure mode for mature Lean transformations seems to be a change in senior leadership to a person who does not believe in Lean or does not understand it. For example, 3M had a renowned innovation engine for many years until James McNerney, an ex-GM executive and Six Sigma aficionado, tried to impose a poorly designed Six Sigma process upon the innovation engine to make it more "efficient" by eliminating "waste"—all the experimental projects that did not turn into products. Instead, 3M's innovation engine sputtered to a halt, and some of its most knowledgeable experts chose to leave rather than tolerate the changes. Product developers know that we need to explore many ideas in order to find the one that will become a great product. These experiments are not waste; in fact, they are the fuel that drives the engine of value creation in an innovation-dependent company. McNerney's successor, George Buckley, had to figure out how to get the innovation engine going again.

START WHEREVER YOU ARE

The only way to become a Lean organization is to begin using Lean Thinking on something that is important to your group.

Start wherever you are, with the problems that are right in front of you, and don't worry too much about picking the right pilot team or the right problems. The first task is to build some direct experience with Lean Product Development, and you can do that by solving almost any problem using Lean practices.

If this is the first book you have ever read about Lean Product Development, you are in phase 0. It's time to do some experimentation and talk about this with your peers to see if you can get them interested. A book study group is a great way to spread your enthusiasm during this stage, and it will build up your personal support network as you begin to ask for official sponsorship. It may also be time to pull together a Lean working group to conduct some small-scale pilots and to begin talking to leaders about the most important problems your organization needs to solve.

Don't spend a lot of time developing a complex architecture for your Lean transformation team; develop the metrics you need as you go along. It's important not to overthink this; your plans will change as you learn more.

Discussion Questions

- Where are you in the four-phase model? What is your logical next step?
- What projects or problems will best support your need to develop some internal success stories to demonstrate that Lean works for your organization?

- Who are the major stakeholders for Lean Product Development? What are their biggest problems and how can Lean Product Development solve them?

Next Actions

- ☐ If you have not already done so, develop a plan to write your first three A3s and then mentor someone in your organization through his or her first A3s.
- ☐ Enlist your allies. Draw up a list of people who are likely to support you on the next stage of your company's journey with Lean product development. Give them this book or another one that has been helpful to you and set up some time to discuss the ideas.
- ☐ With your team, identify the team-level issues that would benefit from some focused problem solving. Set aside some meeting time to work together to solve them.

Epilogue: Just Start Somewhere, Just Do Something

Just start somewhere. Just do something.

Just use LAMDA to solve a problem that is right in front of you.

Lean Product Development is not more complicated than this.

Solving small problems makes it easier to tackle bigger ones. A little waste eliminated frees up time to create more value. The skills that you build solving small problems for yourself will help you tackle larger ones that get in the way of your company's growth. One success builds momentum for others. The most sophisticated Lean Product Development systems began with one small step.

As Lean Product Developers, we know that every problem has an opportunity embedded in it. More problems mean more opportunities for meaningful innovation.

THE LEAN PRODUCT DEVELOPMENT SYSTEM

Allen Ward, Michael Kennedy, and others describe Lean Product Development as a system with elements that work together and reinforce each other: LAMDA, A3s, limit curves, responsibility-based planning, SBCE, and the Chief Engineer all work together to improve the flow of work. In Kennedy's book, *Product Development for the Lean Enterprise,* he states that it is the intersection of four elements in particular (Chief Engineer/system designer, SBCE, responsibility-based planning, and expert engineering workforce) that produce the benefits of Lean. These specific elements are an adaptation of the Toyota Product Development System.

Today, I have observed that this emphasis on the system of Lean Product Development has not been helpful to the community of Lean Product Developers. For one thing, like our Lean Manufacturing colleagues 15 years ago, we focused too much on the observable differences between the Toyota Product Development System and traditional product development. We did not focus enough on the underlying principles that led Toyota to develop this set of countermeasures to solve its specific problems.

We also unwittingly encouraged our audience to see Lean Product Development as "all or nothing": Either embrace the entire system (or at least try) or just forget the entire thing. If senior leadership support cannot be obtained for a massive transformation, Lean has had nothing to say about what should be done instead. I have read in many places that Lean is a long-term commitment, yet it is unreasonable to expect executives to commit to a lengthy initiative without some internal demonstration of likely success. I used to tell my clients that it's useless to implement only one tool from the Lean toolkit; yet, I have seen companies make dramatic improvements in product development by doing exactly that, and I've observed that such a success opens doors for other elements of the system.

Along the way, I have seen a lot of promising work abandoned when managers met practices like the "Chief Engineer" and SBCE with strong resistance. The focus on eliminating waste and maximizing value got lost in some of these battles. I have seen some people achieve great results, but still tell me that their Lean efforts failed because they could not do everything the books told them they should do.

Yet the companies whose stories you just read did not let the problems with the system perspective get in the way of solving the problems that were most important to them. Those kinds of changes tend to stick around long after consultants leave and system-level visions have been abandoned.

MYTHS, LEGENDS, AND STORIES

The truth is that, even in Toyota, we cannot find a single real example that brings this hypothetical system to life. Instead, we have myths and legends. We have the stories of god-like Chief Engineers' heroic journeys to deeply understand customer value. We have the stories of the tough *senseis* who worked with American managers at NUMMI in California and Georgetown, Kentucky, to prove that Americans could replicate Toyota's practices outside Japan—that their methods did not depend upon the homogeneity of Japanese culture. We have the examples of the Lexus and the Prius to show how this can lead to breakthrough products.

Yet Toyota is a problematic example for product developers. Before its struggles, it was known for predictable, reliable products that did not excite anyone the way that Porsches, BMWs, and even Chryslers and Volkswagens could. People drove Toyotas because they were reliable cars. People drive the New Beetles and Mini Coopers because they love those cars.

If it were not for Lean Manufacturing, it is unlikely that anyone would have studied the Toyota Product Development System.

Meanwhile, Steve Jobs at Apple, the geeks in Google Labs, the product champions at 3M, the social anthropologists at IDEO, and social media tycoons have legendary product development tales of their own. These people have figured out how to maximize value and minimize waste— even though they don't use the same words to describe what they do.

When we let go of the need to copy Toyota's observed practices and focus on problem solving to maximize value, Lean gives us the ability to hear the morals embedded in these tales—to see the countermeasures that go against conventional wisdom to revolutionize the core value streams of product development.

THE VALUE EMBEDDED IN MYTHIC SYSTEMS

So if no one's really done it—if all the stuff that's been written about the Lean Product Development system is mythical—what good is it?

It helps to remind us that product development is a complex system, but one that responds in predictable ways to specific countermeasures. The parts of Lean Product Development, as practiced at Toyota, do reinforce each other. If one of Toyota's countermeasures works well at your company, another one may be worth a try. It organizes the experiences that we have to describe the countermeasures that work most often and the ones that did not work. It can serve as a vision while we develop our own.

Our challenge is to make these myths, legends, stories, case studies, and examples actionable for us. We have to take what we can use immediately and do something with it, while we file away the rest to revisit later.

THE REAL-WORLD LEAN PD SYSTEM

None of the companies I've met are finished with Lean Product Development and none of them have a product development system that Allen Ward would recognize as his own. They have taken what they could learn from Toyota and from other places and made the practices work for them. Yet the Lean Product Development systems described in this book had some commonalities:

- The Lean Product Development organization is a team of systematic problem solvers working to deliver more customer value and more business value. They have confidence in their ability to create value, and they see problems and opportunities everywhere. As a result, team members have better ideas and they get those ideas out into the market faster, with much less waste along the way.
- The idea becomes the unit of knowledge—not the product or the platform. The idea can be as simple as a way to reduce the costs of a small fastener or as big as the creation of a new industry. Ideas have recognized value in a Lean Product Development organization, and the raw materials for these ideas—the shared storehouses of knowledge and experiences—are more accessible.
- Waste is intolerable. Lean Product Development clears out the clutter of busywork, boring meetings, and unnecessary reinvention to focus the team's attention on the customer's and the organization's most pressing needs for innovation.
- The most basic tools of Lean Product Development—LAMDA, A3 reports, visual product plans, and Lean meetings—work immediately to surface problems and then find the opportunities that lurk inside them.

In a system like this, innovation is as natural as breathing.

THE MASTERY OF INNOVATION

The mastery of innovation is the ability to solve problems and create knowledge, capitalize on that knowledge, and use it to drive decision making. That gives you the freedom to do things that you were not able to do in the past.

This is what makes a company innovative: the ability to apply its best available knowledge to the best problems to solve. It turns out that we can make innovation predictable, relying less on serendipity, if we have a deep pool of knowledge to draw from and we know how to use it.

Just as Innovation Masters have deep knowledge of their company's technology, customers, and operational processes that they apply to create breakthrough products, you can build deep knowledge of your company's product development system to create your own break-throughs in product development performance, whatever that means to your company.

THE POWER OF MASTERY

Masters have the ability to make the most of whatever materials they have in front of them. Their toolbox is full, with a variety of tools that feel nat-ural in their hands from practiced use. They have the deep knowledge needed to solve the most complex problems in their fields, developing new methods when old ones are not fit for the job.

Masters share knowledge with others. They mentor the apprentices and journeymen, sharing the thinking processes behind their decisions so that their mentees build the ability to solve complex problems on their own. They recognize that written instructions don't tell half the story. They work side by side with members of their teams to develop the base of shared experience, which is the only way to transfer tacit knowledge directly.

With the power of this knowledge, you can tune your product develop-ment process to optimize for the things that are most important to you, and then reoptimize it when it changes. Sometimes, speed is everything. Sometimes, cost is king. Lean helps you get everything you need—but sometimes, not at the same time. Usually, one area comes first and then the rest come around.

The path to mastery starts right where you stand. It doesn't really matter what you do first: visual planning, A3s, obvious waste elimina-tion, or more effective meetings. Make problems visible and then start fixing them.

THE MASTERS OF INNOVATION

The stories in this book show that there is no one right path, no single way to build a Lean Product Development system.

Yet, as I visited these companies and talked with these people, they had a few things in common:

1. They were almost uniformly humble about what they had achieved. This is the humility that comes out in an environment where problems are visible. It's not that things are perfect; in fact, we strive for perfection knowing that we'll never reach it. We see problems everywhere but they no longer have the power to harm us.

2. They had set and achieved measurable results that were important to their organizations' success. Because they had clear targets, their progress toward achieving those results was visible, and because those targets were important, they got done. That helped them overcome the discomfort of change.

3. They figured out what Lean Product Development meant to them—as Aerospace, Pharmaceutical, or Scientific Instrument companies. They kept the word "Lean" to maintain the connection to external practitioner communities they could learn from, but they defined that word for themselves.

4. They tolerated no excuses from themselves or their teams, no matter where they were in the organization's hierarchies. Not everyone in this book was in a traditional leadership role—certainly not at the start. It helps a lot to have leadership support, but they didn't wait until they had it to make the changes that were right in front of them.

5. They started somewhere. They got something done.

Life inside a Lean Product Development organization is not perfect. It's still frustrating sometimes. There is still a lot of friction. In fact, you may be less willing to tolerate waste once you know what it looks like. Since many of the countermeasures of Lean Product Development make problems visible, at first, all you may see are problems. But the problems were there the whole time. Lean has just made them visible. Now that you can see them, you can do something about them.

YOUR FIRST STEPS TOWARD THE MASTERY OF INNOVATION

I've shown you what it has meant to these companies to become a Lean Product Development organization. What would it mean to you?

Before closing this book, go back through the action steps at the end of every chapter. Pick one and put it on your calendar to do tomorrow morning.

Share this book with a few people who can become companions on your journey. Share the discussion questions with them and begin to debate the ideas. Appendix 2 has a book study guide to help you organize a group.

Spend an hour just sitting or wandering around and LOOK at your workplace. What waste do you see? What opportunities to maximize value? What problems to solve?

Just start somewhere. Just do something. Then let us know how it turns out.

Appendix 1: The Mastery of Innovation Self-Assessment

WHERE ARE THE OPPORTUNITIES TO IMPROVE DECISION MAKING?

For each statement, mark the box that shows how much you agree or disagree with it.

No.	Question	Strongly Disagree	Disagree	Neutral	Agree	Strongly Agree
1	When we go into a decision meeting or gate review, we know that the right people will be in the room to make decisions.	_____	_____	_____	_____	_____
2	Managers in my organization ask good, challenging questions when I present my findings and recommendations to them.	_____	_____	_____	_____	_____
3	When I recognize a problem that we have seen before, I have the ability to find out how we solved it last time.	_____	_____	_____	_____	_____
4	We explore multiple alternatives before making key decisions.	_____	_____	_____	_____	_____

No.	Question	Strongly Disagree	Disagree	Neutral	Agree	Strongly Agree
5	The technical staff get regular opportunities to deepen their customer knowledge with early customer feedback on their product designs.	_____	_____	_____	_____	_____
6	Product development programs meet their schedules consistently.	_____	_____	_____	_____	_____
7	Decision makers take the time to understand the problems, alternatives, and recommendations before making a decision.	_____	_____	_____	_____	_____
8	There are few design loopbacks late in development.	_____	_____	_____	_____	_____
9	We take the time to capture what we've learned so that we can share it with others and reuse it ourselves later.	_____	_____	_____	_____	_____
10	We do not hold up the flow of technical work with artificial barriers imposed by the phases and gates on our product development process.	_____	_____	_____	_____	_____
11	We take some time to understand root causes before we recommend countermeasures or solutions.	_____	_____	_____	_____	_____
12	Customers are highly satisfied with our product's quality.	_____	_____	_____	_____	_____
13	When we go into a decision meeting or gate review, we are confident that there will be no last-minute objections or issues to delay decisions.	_____	_____	_____	_____	_____

No.	Question	Strongly Disagree	Disagree	Neutral	Agree	Strongly Agree
14	Managers in my organization use systematic problem solving to solve problems within their span of control.	_____	_____	_____	_____	_____
15	We take the time to identify the people who need to be consulted about a decision, and then engage them in the decision-making process.	_____	_____	_____	_____	_____
16	We take the time to measure results and reflect upon the effectiveness of the decisions that we make so that we can learn.	_____	_____	_____	_____	_____
17	Our groups' leaders do not second guess the decisions they have delegated to their teams.	_____	_____	_____	_____	_____
18	My team's information systems make it easy to find documentation from past projects that could be helpful to me now.	_____	_____	_____	_____	_____
19	We understand what problems we need to solve early in development to minimize technical risk and we solve them before we enter detailed design.	_____	_____	_____	_____	_____
20	We actively search out reusable knowledge and expert input as part of our problem-solving and decision-making processes.	_____	_____	_____	_____	_____

No.	Question	Strongly Disagree	Disagree	Neutral	Agree	Strongly Agree
21	We know what our customers will pay for our products and we have the ability to design our products to cost targets that maximize value for our customers and profits for our organization.	_____	_____	_____	_____	_____
22	We know who has the authority to make the important decisions in our organization.	_____	_____	_____	_____	_____
23	We have the ability to kill a product development program in early development when it becomes clear that the product won't meet its goals.	_____	_____	_____	_____	_____
24	We have the capacity to deliver the products needed to achieve our organization's growth targets without overloading development resources or adding additional staff.	_____	_____	_____	_____	_____

WHAT PATTERNS DO YOU OBSERVE?

Score 1 point for each "strongly disagree," 2 for "agree," 3 for "neutral," 4 for "agree," and 5 for "strongly agree."

> **Questions 6, 8, 24: Resource maximization: ability to optimize capacity, development resources, and time to market.**
> Max: 15
> Your score: _____

Questions 5, 12, 21: Customer value: ability to maximize customer value, including benefits, quality, and cost.
Max: 15
Your score: _____

Questions 4, 7, 11, 16, 19: Systematic problem solving: ability to use problem-solving methods that solve problems systematically and permanently.
Max: 25
Your score: _____

Questions 1, 10, 13, 15, 23: Effective decision making: ability to make decisions that deliver the expected results without being revisited or causing unintended side effects.
Max: 25
Your score: _____

Questions 3, 9, 18, 20: Knowledge capture and reuse: ability to maximize value from the organization's knowledge.
Max: 20
Your score: _____

Questions 2, 14, 17, 22: Support to grow problem-solving skills: ability to support each other and coach development staff to build problem-solving ability in every member of the team.
Max: 20
Your score: _____

RECOMMENDATIONS

Each product development organization has unique circumstances that make general recommendations based on a simple questionnaire highly speculative. My experience has shown that there are some general patterns.

Resource maximization is the ability to optimize capacity, development resources, and time to market.

- If you scored medium to low on this dimension (3–9), then Lean Product Development practices like rapid learning cycles, visual management, and convergent decision making will improve the flow of work to help you eliminate the root causes of schedule delays, overloaded resources, and insufficient R & D capacity.
- If you scored high on this dimension (10–15) but you scored low on customer value, then you will benefit more from practices that will help you apply systematic problem solving more rigorously to deepen technical and customer knowledge.
- If you scored medium to low on both dimensions, mastering the foundational Lean Product Development practices of rapid learning cycles, visual management, and effective decisions will help you improve both dimensions at once.

Customer value is the ability to maximize customer value, including benefits, quality, and cost.

- If you scored medium to low on this dimension (3–9), then Lean Product Development practices like voice-of-the-customer, design for Lean, reusable knowledge capture, and target costing will help you deliver more customer and business value in your products.

The final four dimensions assess your current capabilities with the foundational practices of Lean Product Development. Many organizations score low to medium on all four dimensions when they start with Lean Product Development. These groups get results the fastest when they select pilot teams to experiment with foundational Lean Product Development practices like LAMDA, A3 thinking, visual management, and nemawashi. The pilot teams build internal proofs that Lean Product Development works and, once these practices have been proven, it is much easier to get widespread adoption.

Systematic problem solving is the ability to use problem solving methods that solve problems systematically and permanently.

- If you scored medium to low on this dimension (3–9) but higher on the other dimensions, the ability to solve problems systematically using tools like LAMDA and A3 thinking forms the foundation for advanced Lean Product Development practices like convergent decision making.

Effective decision making is the ability to make decisions that deliver the expected results without being revisited or causing unintended side effects.

- If you scored medium to low on this dimension (3–9) but higher on the others, then Lean meeting practices, nemawashi, visual management, and A3 reports will help you leverage your strengths in these other areas into your decision making.

Knowledge capture and reuse is the ability to maximize value from the organization's knowledge.

- If you scored medium to low on this dimension (3–9) but higher on the others, then learning how to recognize, capture, and share reusable knowledge will help you get more value from the solutions you develop and the decisions that you make so that you do not solve the same problems over and over.

Support to grow problem-solving skills is the ability to support each other and coach development staff to build problem-solving ability in every member of the team.

- If you scored medium to low on this dimension (3–9) but higher on the others, then learning how to serve as a coach and mentor will help you share your problem-solving and decision-making strengths with the other members of your organization.

Appendix 2: A Guide for Book Study Groups

When I asked the companies I visited for my field research how they got started with Lean, many of them mentioned that they had either organized or participated in a book study group that got together regularly to discuss a reading from one of the books available about Lean Product Development.

These groups helped create momentum for change, by providing the participants with some time to reflect upon the new ideas they found in their book and to explore ways that the ideas could help their organization. Often these study groups led to individual experimentation with the practices and then to pilot groups and, ultimately, to organization-wide programs.

HOW TO USE THIS BOOK IN A STUDY GROUP

This book has been informed by my case study sponsors' experiences with book study groups. Each chapter includes Discussion Questions that your group can use to jump-start discussion, as well as Next Actions to provide some ideas for how to begin experimenting with Lean Product Development.

- Make a list of people who might join you and then ask them if they would be interested. Look for people who naturally seek to improve how the organization does its work and who are willing to experiment with new ideas. List more people than you need—at least 15.
- Ask them whether or not they would be interested in reading this book as part of a study group. Include a link to the Amazon page for this book or the supplemental website page that includes the list of case studies.
- Once you have at least six people, schedule the first meeting and order the books. If everyone says yes, you may end up with too many for one group. Break it into two or more smaller ones.

- Schedule a conference room that has at least one flip chart for taking notes and a whiteboard. Chapter reviews should not be so formal that they require a projector.
- At the first meeting, pass out the books and agree upon the meeting schedule, reading assignments, chapter report assignments, and group ground rules and expectations. You may decide that the group will keep discussions confidential, will not bring laptops, etc. Set the rules you need to make sure that the meetings stay focused and on track.
- Take action right away if someone misses more than one meeting so that the group doesn't lose momentum. As the organizer, it's your responsibility to check in when people go missing. If the group isn't working for someone, it's better to let him or her go gracefully so that everyone else is not distracted by the absences.
- After you have finished the book, hold one final meeting to reflect upon the group's experience. They may want to tackle another book or they may want to take some group action to put the ideas into place.
- Celebrate! Do something special to bring the group to a good conclusion.

BEST PRACTICES FROM THE FIELD RESEARCH

The people who organized these groups shared a number of ideas about how to run these groups effectively:

Keep reading assignments short and focused. There is no way to sugar-coat this: Book study groups are extra work. Even if you have a powerfully motivated group, it's important to keep the assignments bite-sized. Not only does that make it easier to get the readings done, it also makes it easier to reflect and internalize the things you learned from the reading as the group discusses them. In this book, one chapter per session will be about right.

Keep chapter reports informal and discussion based. Please don't assign an A3 report on every chapter. We're not in 7th grade English class. It is helpful to assign someone to facilitate the study group meetings, but he or she should summarize the main ideas on a flip chart and then generate some discussion questions for the group to consider. I have included some suggestions at the end of each chapter, and the facilitator may want to add one or two that are specific to your company.

Meet on a regular schedule and commit to attending each meeting. These groups thrive on consistency and a regular cadence of meetings. They can be weekly, biweekly, or monthly depending upon how intensely the group wants to work together. Being human, some people will read the assignment the day before the meeting no matter how much time there is between them, and others will read the whole book because it's interesting. These groups fall apart when attendance is inconsistent or people come unprepared. Erratic attendance drains away the group's momentum. Group members need to commit to every meeting unless there is a true emergency, or they let group members know in advance that they have a conflict. They need to have done the reading when they arrive.

Keep the groups small and closed. These groups help build momentum because they help create strong relationships and a shared base of experience among a group of potential Lean Product Development leaders. That starts to break down once the group number gets larger than 12, or if group membership changes too often. Close the group to new members after the first three meetings. Larger groups can be broken down into small ones, and latecomers can be encouraged to organize their own groups.

Do something together to make the new ideas actionable. Each meeting can end with the commitment to take action, either individually or as a group. The actions might be to test out one of the ideas from the book, to spend some time observing the organization, or to identify and eliminate an obvious source of unnecessary waste. They don't have to be large actions to get the ball rolling. Small ones add up.

AFTER YOU FINISH THE BOOK STUDY, WHAT NEXT?

At the companies I talked with, book study groups enlisted product development leadership, recruited and supported pilot teams, built and delivered training programs, and mentored others in problem-solving skills.

Chances are that your own group will have developed lots of ideas for next steps and will have already begun to experiment with the foundational practices and countermeasures. I would encourage you to keep the group together as an advisory board to help shape your organization's next steps with Lean Product Development. The group may not need to meet as often. By now, you should know which members are fully on board and which ones are still skeptical. The enthusiastic supporters keep you going and the skeptics keep you honest.

Good luck, Godspeed, and let me know how things work out!

Appendix 3: List of Participating Companies

A-Dec
> Headquartered in: Newburg, Oregon
> Annual revenue: $268 million (2010)
> Number of employees: 980
> Industry: Dental Equipment

Buckeye Technologies
> Headquartered in: Memphis, Tennessee
> Annual revenue: $940 million (2011)
> Number of employees: 1,400
> Industry: Pulp and Paper

DJO Global
> Headquartered in: Vista, California
> Annual revenue: $1.08 billion (2011)
> Number of employees: 6,000
> Industry: Medical Devices

Ford Motor Company
> Headquartered in: Dearborn, Michigan
> Annual revenue: $136 billion (2011)
> Number of employees: 164,000
> Industry: Automotive

Goodyear Tire Company
> Headquartered in: United States
> Annual revenue: $22.9 billion (2011)
> Number of employees: 73,000
> Industry: Automotive

Hixson
Headquartered in: Cincinnati, Ohio
Annual revenue: not disclosed
Number of employees: not disclosed
Industry: Architectural and Engineering Services

Irwin Seating Company
Headquartered in: Grand Rapids, Michigan
Annual revenue: not disclosed
Number of employees: 600
Industry: Architectural Products

Metsec
Headquartered in: Oldsbury, West Midlands, United Kingdom
Annual revenue: £100 million (2011)
Number of employees: 200
Industry: Industrial Products

Nielsen-Kellerman
Headquartered in: Boothwyn, Pennsylvania
Annual revenue: $12 million (2011)
Number of employees: 80
Industry: Handheld Electronics

Novo Nordisk
Headquartered in: Basel, Switzerland
Annual revenue: $11 billion (2011)
Number of employees: 32,700
Industry: Pharmaceuticals

Playworld Systems
Headquartered in: Lewisburg, Pennsylvania
Annual revenue: undisclosed
Number of employees: 200
Industry: Playground Equipment

Royal Philips Company

Headquartered in: Amsterdam, the Netherlands
Annual revenue: €22.6 billion (2011)
Number of employees: 122,000
Industry: Consumer Electronics

RUAG

Headquartered in: Bern, Switzerland
Annual revenue: CHF 1.7 billion (2011)
Number of employees: 7,700
Industry: Aerospace

Scania

Headquartered in: Södertälje, Sweden
Annual revenue: SEK 9.4 billion (2011)
Number of employees: 37,500
Industry: Automotive

Steelcase

Headquartered in: Grand Rapids, Michigan
Annual revenue: $2.4 billion (2011)
Number of employees: 10,000
Industry: Office Furniture

Unger Marketing, Inc.

Headquartered in: Bridgeport, Connecticut
Annual revenue: not disclosed
Number of employees: not disclosed
Industry: Cleaning Products

Vaisala

Headquartered in: Vantaa, Finland
Annual revenue: €201 million (2011)
Number of employees: 1,400
Industry: Scientific Instruments

Visteon

Headquartered in: Copenhagen, Denmark
Annual revenue: $8 billion (2011)
Number of employees: 26,000
Industry: Automotive

Watlow

Headquartered in: St. Louis, Missouri
Annual revenue: $330 million
Number of employees: 2,400
Industry: Industrial Electronics

Appendix 4: Suggested Reading List and Other Resources

THE LEAN PRODUCT DEVELOPMENT RESOURCE CENTER

The Lean Product Development Resource Center is a free, online source of information for Lean product developers. It includes how-to articles, templates, examples, and guidelines for how to put the practices in this book into action (http://lpdrc.com).

ARTICLES

Radeka, K., and T. Sutton. 2007. What is lean about product development? *Vision Magazine,* Product Development Management Association, June 2007.

Sobek, D. K., J. K. Liker, and A. C. Ward. 1998. Another look at how Toyota integrates product development. *Harvard Business Review* 76 (4) 36–50.

Sobek, D. K., A. C. Ward, and J. K. Liker. 1999. Toyota's principles of set-based concurrent engineering. *Sloan Management Review* 40 (2): 67–83

Ward, A. C., D. K. Sobek, J. K. Liker, and J. J. Christiano. 1995. The second Toyota paradox: How delaying decisions can make better cars faster. *Sloan Management Review* 36 (3): 43–61.

BOOKS

Flinchbauch, J., and A. Carlino. 2006. *The hitchhiker's guide to lean.* Society of Manufacturing Engineers. ISBN 0872638316.

Kennedy, M. N. 2003. *Product development for the lean enterprise.* Richmond, VA: Oaklea Press. ISBN 1892538091.

Liker, J. K. 2004. *The Toyota way.* New York: McGraw-Hill. ISBN 0071392319.

Mascitelli, R. 2011. *Mastering lean product development.* Northridge, CA: Technology Perspectives. ISBN 0966269748.

Morgan, J. M., and J. K. Liker. 2006. *The Toyota product development system.* New York: Productivity Press. ISBN 1563272822.

Nonaka, I., and H. Takeuchi. 1995. *The knowledge-creating company.* Oxford University Press. ISBN 0195092694.

Poppendieck, M., and T. Poppendieck. 2003. *Lean software development.* Boston, MA: Addison-Wesley. ISBN 0321150783.

Reinertsen, D. 1997. *Managing the design factory.* New York: Free Press. ISBN 0684839911.

———. 2009. *The principles of product development flow.* Redondo Beach, CA: Celeritas Publishing. ISBN 1935401009.

Schipper, T., and M. Swets. 2009. *Innovative lean development.* New York: Productivity Press. ISBN 1420092987.

Sobek, D. K., II, and A. Smalley. 2008. *Understanding A3 thinking.* New York: Productivity Press. ISBN 1563273608.

Ward, A. C. 2007. *Lean product & process development.* Cambridge, MA: Lean Enterprise Institute. ISBN 1934109134.

Womack, J., and D. T. Jones. 2002. *Lean thinking*, 2nd ed. New York: Free Press. ISBN 0743249275.

Womack, J., D. T. Jones, and D. Roos. 1990. *The machine that changed the world.* New York: Harper Perennial. ISBN 0060974176.

Index

About the Author

Katherine Radeka has a rare combination of business acumen, scientific depth, and the ability to untangle the organizational knots to remove the barriers to change. In the past seven years, her consulting firm, Whittier Consulting Group, Inc., has engaged with clients such as Steelcase, Hewlett-Packard, and more than 50 other leading organizations.

In 2010 and 2011, Katherine conducted the Lean Product Development Benchmarking Study to document Lean Product Development practices at more than 60 companies in North America and Europe. In 2005, she logged more than 11,000 miles driving around the country to research how the best companies got more ROI from product development. In 2007, she cofounded the Lean Product & Process Development Exchange, a nonprofit organization to promote the use of Lean Thinking to improve ROI from product development.

Katherine has climbed seven of the tallest peaks in the Cascade Mountains and spent 10 days alone on the Pacific Crest Trail until an encounter with a bear convinced her that she needed a change in strategic direction.